TABLE OF CONTENTS

THE PROBLEM

Have you ever pushed and pushed to make the best gains possible at something … only to look up one day and find yourself stuck on a plateau … a place of zero improvement—no matter how hard you try? Ask any athlete, they know all about plateaus. Like spending endless hours in the gym, without seeing any gains.

These flat, dry places seem to last forever, especially in painting. I know, because I've been there as an artist. The good news is there's an answer, something you can do to leave an art plateau far behind.

Many years ago I watched in wonder as new energy and life was breathed into my paintings. My hope is that what follows will do the same for you—and more.

This book will cover how that magic came to be—accidently. Because of that, what follows will be an account of how I stumbled my way toward understanding outdoor painting, which I finally did. So for some, this book is a great "how-to" manual using Plein Air (a French expression for: in the open air) painting to improve as an artist.

Lastly, for a rare few, it'll be something beyond a book on art. It'll be a story about the pursuit of artistic excellence that, over time, reveals some basic truths regarding success in general. Seven in all, that if applied properly, can take you almost anywhere you'd like to go.

THE INTRODUCTION

Feeling stalled as an artist, like you're in a creative slump?
I've been there. Years ago, I desperately sought to improve as an
oil painter—nothing seemed to work. I was stuck. Then, with some
help from one of America's top illustrators, a door opened for me.
What followed was a breathtaking season of growth that propelled
me forward as an artist.

The ultimate goal? For you to emerge as a better, bolder, and
more confident artist. While the techniques predominantly focus
on oil paints, I believe they can be readily adapted for use with
watercolors. Fair warning: this process will require something
special from you. It's meant for those who are willing to put in the
time and effort to be their very best. I have placed some reference
links throughout this book to help you. When you see a link,
simply flip to the back of the book and scan the QR code to take
you there.

I should add that the journey shared within these pages changed
me forever as an artist, playing a pivotal role in my transition
to becoming a full-time professional. So, if you've been feeling
creatively stagnant, it's time to roll up your sleeves. You can do
this! Deep down, you're a much better artist than you think!

THE 7 STEPS ...

1. Have a destination ... in short, a goal.
2. Learn all you can about how to get there, and how others
    have made it
3. Get in shape for the trip
4. Make the preparatory exercises harder than the actual trip
5. Increase your failure rate during the exercises—stretch
    yourself
6. Begin seeing yourself & how it would feel to successfully
    get there
7. Don't give up

The 7 Steps didn't show up for me in that exact order. During
the original process everything was messy, painful and terribly
unclear. Like so many things in life, clarity settled in after the
struggle. So please be patient while I do my best to fit the 7 Steps
into what follows.

Notes

CHAPTER 1

Finding My Way...

*Don't wish it were easier,
wish you were better!*

– EARL SHOAF –

THE BEGINNING OF A SOLUTION

It all began one day about 30 years ago with what seemed at the time like some pretty simple advice. It was so simple in fact that I almost blew it off. What gave it weight was who'd said it. It came from a former top New York illustrator—Tom Ryan. Tom had moved out West, and was busy creating some of the finest Cowboy paintings in the world. So when we talked, I listened—closely.

I had no idea then, but the door that Tom cracked open for me that day would eventually lead me on a journey ... a very long journey

GETTING BETTER ~~CAN BE~~ **IS** HARD WORK!

It's important to say, right up front with no apologies, this isn't for everyone. This is for the adventurous at heart, the gutsy ones … the ones that HAVE TO KNOW just how good they can become as an artist. I know that may sound a bit pretentious to some, but it's true.

Ask yourself, just how big is your artistic gift? Yes … I personally believe it's a gift you have. I'll bet it's bigger than you think. What are your limits? Just how good can you become as an artist? Honestly, nobody knows. But you can work to find out.

Like so many other things, if you *really* want it to happen, it's going to take some serious effort on your part. That shouldn't really be a surprise. Excellence and lasting gains *always* require that kind of commitment. Just decide you're going to give it everything you've got, right here, right now. Most won't do it. But for those special few that do commit, I'm betting you'll be astonished at where you end up as an artist.

THE FIRST DOMINO

Here's what Tom Ryan told me that day …
"What you really need to do is start painting outdoors. Keep the paintings small … 8"x10" or so … and don't spend more than about half an hour on each one. It's all out there; the truth is right in front of you outdoors. Keep at it until they look pretty good after 30 minutes".

That's it. That's the advice Tom gave me that day. Seems pretty straight forward. I mean, go outside and paint for half an hour? BIG DEAL! I can do that. How tough can it be? (I'm smiling as I write this; later on you'll read about my catastrophic first attempt).

The truth is: Tom had pushed that "first domino" in me …
the single, initial domino that caused a zillion other dominoes
to fall over in spellbinding succession.

ARE WE GAINING OR LOSING?

It's important to recognize that none of us remain in 100%
stasis, a state of zero change. Whether we realize it or not, each
of us is ALWAYS in flux. This is especially true when it comes to
something requiring a specialized skill like painting. We're either
gaining or losing some hard-to-measure quantity of our unique
painting ability each and every day. Sorry, but it's true.

This basic truth applies to everyone, not just artists. Noteworthy
others include: professional athletes, top musicians and world
class public speakers. I mention that here, because if we take the
offensive and focus ourselves on constant improvement,
there's far less risk of ever losing ground.

But the question then arises, at least it did for me before
Tom stepped in: How do we improve and *keep* improving as
artists? How can we avoid plateaus and keep the gains coming?
Workshops? Books (like this one)? Art classes? YouTube videos?
Private instruction?

I've done them all, and they've usually helped me improve
to some degree. But as good as those things can be at times,
in comparison, I've personally found that their results can be
sporadic and unreliable over the long haul.

Here's the deal; I know this to work. I've seen the powerful
results show up in my own life. Constant gains. I'm not saying
I'm the world's greatest artist. I *am* saying I'm personally a better

artist this year than I was last year ... and the year before, and so on. When is comes to improvement, the only real competition we have is with ourselves!

Dreams without goals remain dreams.
– DENZEL WASHINGTON –

One of the biggest takeaways from this book should be the principle: Set Goals to improve—and you will. (I did!)

So begin setting yourself daily goals, weekly goals, monthly goals, yearly goals... you get the idea. If you want to turn your dreams into reality, set goals on how you plan to get there. E.g. "I'm going to do five timed, small paintings this week".

Notes

Notes

This ISN'T regular Plein Air painting!

Things aren't always what they seem

– PHAEDRUS –

OKAY, SO YOU'RE GOING TO PAINT OUTDOORS. HOWEVER…
<u>YOU'RE NOT GOING TO BE LIKE EVERYONE ELSE THAT'S
PAINTING OUTSIDE</u>

When all this took place, there were darn few outdoor
(or *Plein Air*) painters. That's all changed. Now a TON of people
are outside painting. Honestly, I think that's great—Plein Air
painting is fun!

It's important to understand, what I'm proposing here may LOOK
like normal *Plein Air* painting, but it's not—not really. There are
radical differences between what I'll be taking you through and
what most outdoor painters are out doing.

To help make my point, here's an account of my first (disastrous) time painting outdoors as I tried my best to follow Tom's advice.

HERE WE GO …

A small white canvas panel was tightly clamped onto my brand new French easel; piles of paint were carefully set out just right on the palette. Several professional-grade brushes were in hand … everything was ready!

I picked up my small digital timer, set it to 30-minutes, took a deep breath … and hit the timer's green START button.

I felt a rush of adrenaline! There I was, standing out in the middle of nowhere—alone—trying to do a dumb little oil painting, and my heart was racing. How silly is that? Of course all that pulse pounding was self-induced. I think it's because I'd put so much pressure on myself that THIS WAS IT! <u>THE WAY</u> to become a better painter! Tom Ryan said so!

Of course it wasn't much help that I'd spent ZERO time getting to know my brand new outdoor gear, or that I was in a strange setting … full of a hundred variables like intermittent clouds, wind gusts, winged insects, moving shadows and so on. (Did I mention it was all brand new?)

I IMMEDIATELY began to struggle terribly, in every way imaginable. It was awful. This was NOT easy. I thank God Almighty that nobody was watching back then, because it was all pretty embarrassing. I was absolutely clueless. This was, of course, all pre-YouTube where I could've watched a few videos and picked up some pointers beforehand.

Here's a quick look at the running narrative going on inside my head right after the timer began its merciless 30-minute countdown:

Okay, which brush should I use? Is there a better way to hold it, so I can paint faster? Uh-Oh … the paint's going on way too thin and the color's completely DEAD! Now where did I clip my turp cup? There it is! Oh no, my palette's sliding around every time I use my brush to reach for paint … gotta fix that! Should I be using some sort of painting medium? Might speed things up. The height of the canvas panel sure feels too low on the easel. Wow, those shadows are moving—FAST! Uh-Oh, the wind's starting to blow my stuff all around … on and on it went while I struggled to paint.

Then suddenly, right smack-dab in the middle of this outdoor train wreck, I heard the little white kitchen timer beep out a 10-minute warning. I thought NOOOOO!!! That dumb timer's messed up! That's impossible!! That's waaaay too soon! You mean there's only 10 minutes left to finish this painting?!! I glanced at my wristwatch—and the timer was right. Somehow 20-minutes … now 21-minutes … had blown by!

I immediately started trying to work faster. Then, after what felt like 60-seconds, it beeped out a 5-minute warning. Terror doesn't quite describe what I felt right then, but it's close. I redoubled my efforts. After what seemed like mere moments, I heard the timer's final beeps. My sketch looked timid, lifeless and bland.

So … my first attempt at giving Tom's "simple" advice a try had ended. Honestly, I felt a little wrung out … like I'd been running laps for my High School football coach.

I went and sat down and thought: this is nothing like I'd imagined. After awhile I finally got up, cleaned everything up the best I could, put it in my car and headed for home. There was a LOT to think about ...

DIFFERENCES BETWEEN US AND YOUR AVERAGE OUTDOOR PAINTER

- It's important to keep emphasizing I jumped into this outdoor gig as a way to leave a plateau, improve my studio paintings, and ultimately become a working professional (which I eventually did)—period. This was *never* meant to be an end in itself. This wasn't "the joy of painting nature" stuff ... at least not for some time. It was a pathway, a method. Most *Plein Air* painting is meant to be fun. This wasn't fun, it wasn't supposed to be; this was work—*hard* work. I felt like Tom had given me a secret membership to a hardcore art gym.

- This wasn't a social event, which many *Plein Air* painting sessions can become. That's not a criticism. I'm just trying to draw a practical distinction between the two here. When the timer's ticking away, I can't, *I won't*, stop and visit with ANYONE!

- For the sake of efficiency, I'd pick one location where I could go and paint day after day, week after week—and stay there for months. I wasn't out looking for the next "ideal spot" to paint each time I went out. This was all business.

- Many *Plein Air* painters would never dream of throwing a small painting away. I threw TONS of mine away! Odd as it may seem, discarding a bad oil sketch became an important part of improving.

- There was *always* pressure. Faster, better, bolder …
  push the absolute limits each and every day! Failure is a
  necessary component of ramping up the growth process.
  Does that sound like a relaxing time enjoying the wonders
  of nature?

- Many outdoor painters have their artistic progress a
  bit upside down. "Make the best painting possible, and
  hopefully I'll improve." Painting (a masterpiece) primary,
  me (improving) secondary. Our overarching goal is to work
  harder on YOU as an artist, than on your painting. It really
  comes down to mental priorities. Sure, give it everything
  you've got each time you paint. And yes, try and create a
  30-minute masterpiece, *but keep yourself focused on where
  each 30-minute workout is taking you!* Step-by-step, day
  after day, learn something from each failure and success.
  If you make you the product, then as you improve—every
  future painting will improve as well.

AS A LITTLE ENCOURAGEMENT, HERE'S A LIST OF THE UNEXPECTED BENEFITS THAT BEGAN TO SHOW UP

Note: I'll be going into greater detail on some of these items later, but for right now...

- *I began to paint more intuitively, more creatively—more
  "Right Brain".* Those short, timed, painting sessions
  denied me time to analyze each and every paint stroke—
  especially near the end. Those last wild ten minutes
  were constantly triggering a creative shift day after day.
  I could actually feel it when it would happen. It was like
  I'd suddenly start painting beyond my normal ability and
  limitations.

- *I began taking chances while painting that I'd never dreamt of before.* The short timed painting sessions continually pressured me to make bolder, gutsier brush strokes.

- *I became less petty, more durable—more "bulletproof".* As time passed, my weekly (usually five) half-hour painting sessions quickly began rounding out my corners as a painter. I became less fragile as an artist. Everything didn't have to be perfect. Outdoors, things would go wrong nearly every day. I'd do my best to overcome whatever was thrown at me; then show up all over again the following day for more.

- *Fear of change and experimentation went out the window.* It became relatively easy to experiment with different colors, mediums, palette knives, brushes, textures and techniques. Just slide something new into the schedule and go for it. Fail forward.

- *Everything was accelerated.* Completing five paintings each week, or twenty a month radically upped my personal production. Yes they were small, but many of the same artistic hurdles are always present, regardless of canvas size. This, in turn, accelerated my artistic growth rate. If I happened to crash doing a piece on Wednesday, I'd learn what NOT to do the next day—Thursday. If Thursday happened to be a success in some way, I'd put that positive info to work the following day—Friday. The learning curve suddenly got *really* short.

- *The overall process became easier.* Pulling the gear out, walking to the site, setting up to paint, painting (quickly!), then taking everything down, etc. became super easy over time ... virtually automatic. The process of doing a painting just wasn't a big deal anymore.

- *My understanding of composition and color improved dramatically.* Because I was continually experimenting with compositions as well, I soon learned what designs worked and which ones didn't.

- *Studio paintings soon moved at a faster, more confident pace* ... painting two hours indoors began to feel like an eternity!

In closing here, you probably won't be surprised to hear I eventually started painting plein air just for fun. It just happened over time. No merciless timer, no pressure ... just me out having a good time. It was a nice break. Eventually, any Saturday or Sunday might have me hours from home, standing somewhere gorgeous—painting.

These regular Plein Air paintings were meant to be enjoyable escapes ... a welcome break, where more time could be spent on a piece (or pieces) and it was okay. Many of those small, just-for-fun pieces would later find their way into a San Diego gallery, and sold internationally.

Notes

CHAPTER 3

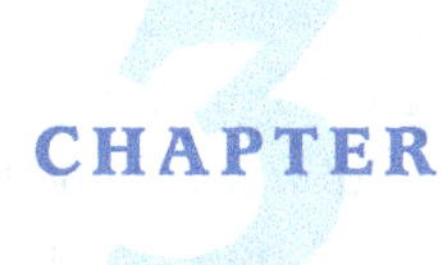

The Gear – Only The Best!

*Never let your materials beat you! You might have
a lousy day one day; maybe you got up on the wrong side of
the bed. Whatever, you're just having one of those bad days.
You can't always control things like that. But you can control
your materials. So do yourself a favor and always buy
the best paint, brushes, etc. that you can.*

– ALEX CHIDICHIMO –

*(The practical truth is: no field ready gear—no painting outdoors.
You'll need specialized equipment to take up the challenge.
This chapter is easily the longest. I should add there was a LOT
of suffering to find out what actually worked.)*

MY FIRST PIECE OF GEAR

After Tom's advice, I raced home and immediately picked up a
genuine Jullian French easel for around $350, the going price back
then. Yep, it looks identical (to me) to a genuine Jullian French
easel selling for roughly half of that today.

Well crafted and rugged, it was very much the standard outdoor easel back then. Honestly, it remains a remarkable design. I can still recall, how after loading it up with painting stuff I felt like I was carrying around my entire studio with me.

I shoved everything I thought I'd need for my first outdoor painting into it, and then boldly and naively headed for the nearby mountains for that first outdoor experience (disaster) I shared earlier.

Over time, I began applying Alex's *"only the best"* (quoted above) mindset to nearly everything, not just paint and materials. I wanted virtually every aspect or item fully optimized. In the end, nothing escaped attention … multi-tool, tripod, backpack, socks, boots, hat, pochade box, umbrella … you name it. Even the small stuff eventually became the best I could buy, make or have made.

It's also important that you know the equipment listed in this chapter took time to develop—years in some cases. So please understand right up front that what's presented here, is far beyond what anyone needs to get started.

If you want to get serious, it'll take a serious investment of not just time—but money. I provide beginners with a "Bare-Bones List" later on. The point is: use whatever makes sense for you, and ignore the rest. Some items easily qualify as overkill.

Looking back, I have to say the endless trial and error, unavoidable mistakes and painful testing to find out what worked and what didn't, was pretty discouraging at the beginning. But then, over time (and with a little help) things *slowly* began to improve.

Step 2

Learn all you can about how to get there.
– FIND YOUR HEROES –

The Bad News (for me) is that open-air landscape artists were pretty rare back when I set out to do all of this. Sure, there were a handful of great outdoor painters back then, but none nearby. E.g. John Stobart, Clark Hulings or Richard Schmid.

The Good News (for me) was that about 70 years earlier some of the greatest Plein Air artists that ever lived had been So. Californians: *Granville Redmond, Edgar Payne, William Wendt* and *Hanson Puthuff*—just to name a few.

Laguna Beach (roughly 90mins from my home) had functioned as an epicenter for a bunch of **Early California Impressionists** (ECI) from about 1900 to 1940.

About the same time I began this process, a wonderful thing happened—*THE ENTIRE WORLD rediscovered these long forgotten impressionist outdoor masters.*

That immediately caused bunches of books to be printed about them (Yay!); museums eagerly pulled out long stored *ECI* paintings for gala functions; specialized art galleries popped up selling ONLY *ECI* work … and so on. One gallery owner at the time told me Early California Impressionist paintings were "the hottest art in the world".

This great awakening couldn't have happened at a better time. I didn't even know they existed. But like a lot of folks, once I saw their work I was hooked.

These brilliant deceased artists instantly became my heroes. I gobbled up their books, traveled to a bunch of museums and countless galleries displaying their paintings.

I even sought out (& received) permission from LACMA *(Los Angeles County Museum of Art)* to paint an oil study (in the museum) from a Granville Redmond in their collection.

I cannot overstate the impact they had on me. They became priceless guides and counselors on how I should tackle outdoor painting.

Oh yeah! If you happen to feel that your outdoor painting gear is already dialed in, please feel free to skip ahead to the next chapter.

I NEED SOME HELP!!!

After further catastrophes outdoors, I caved and reluctantly sought help from Alex Chidichimo, a former instructor of mine (and commercial artist out of Chicago) living in San Diego at the time. I knew he'd give me grief about my "mission" from Tom Ryan, but I didn't care.

A no-nonsense, hard-nosed professional, Alex made it clear he thought I was *completely* wasting my time painting outside, saying more than once, "ALL great art is made in the studio!" I politely listened, but was committed to giving Tom's advice a real chance. So I respectfully ignored his negative comments … and patiently waited for his help.

THE POCHADE BOX

He finally said, "Okay, if you're determined to go outside and paint, get rid of that heavy French easel (it *was* heavy!) and get one of these". He turned for a moment, grabbed something off a nearby cabinet and then faced me holding a small wooden box. It was almost identical in size and shape to an old-fashioned cigar box.

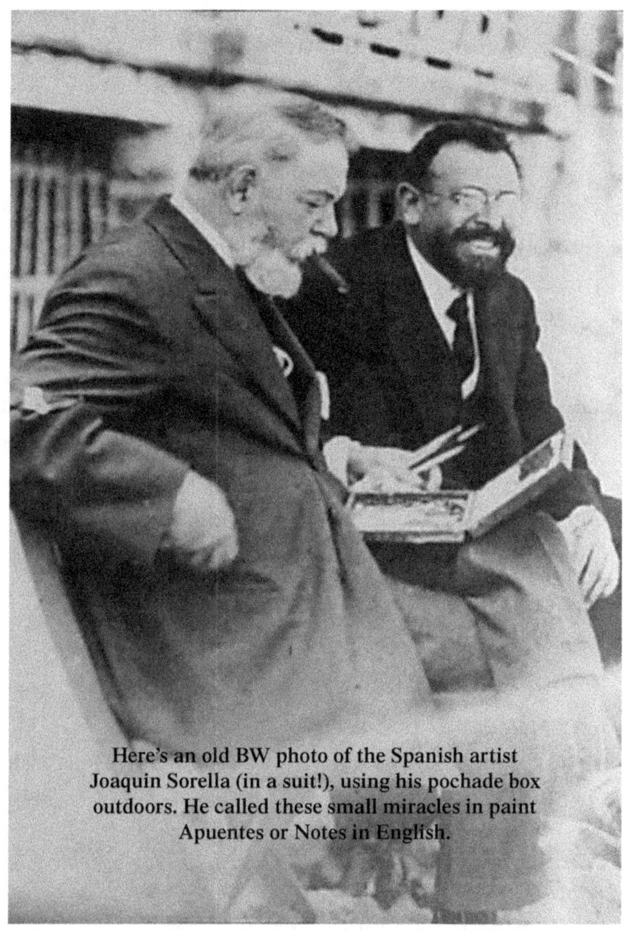

Here's an old BW photo of the Spanish artist Joaquin Sorella (in a suit!), using his pochade box outdoors. He called these small miracles in paint Apuentes or Notes in English.

Handing it to me, he said, "This is what Sorolla used for *his* outdoor studies. It's called a pochade (pō-shawd) box. It's lightweight, compact and far better for what you're trying to do."

Raising its outer lid revealed a small, hinged palette in the lower section, and small clips located up in the lid to hold a small canvas there. Lifting up the leading edge of the tiny palette revealed miniature oil paint tubes, arranged neatly below.

I'd never seen anything like it. Man, did it look COOL! I said, "What about a stand for it?" He turned it over and showed me a small hole located dead center on its underside with metal threads in it. "You can mount a tripod right here". I thought … WOW! Amazing!

He smiled after seeing my reaction, then reached for something nearby and handed me another small wooden box identical to his—but brand new and empty. Then he said, "It's yours. Now get outta here!"

Over the next week I tried to outfit the box just like Alex's and began using it on a daily basis, instead of the French easel. As time passed, I found myself forever trying to make my little pochade box better. I'd go out, use it in the field, then come home and fiddle with it again and again … pursuing "pochade perfection".

Photos of that first, experimental pochade box can be found in *The Viewfinder* section.

I loved that darn thing, but decided I needed something a little bit bigger … one that could handle 9"x12" panels. An ad in the Classifieds of an art magazine offered custom-made pochade boxes out of Massachusetts. I contacted the manufacturer, told him what I wanted

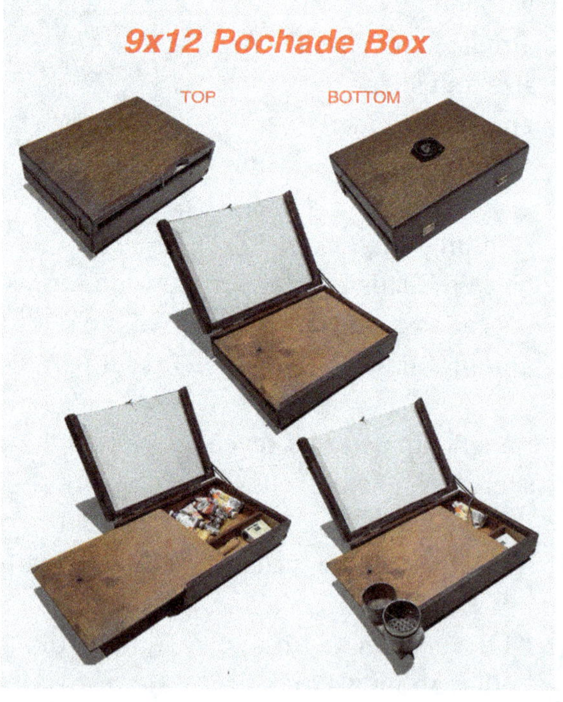

and he built the box I still use today.

Though its corners are worn, it still slides nicely into my backpack, holds a couple canvas panels snuggly in its lid and sets up in moments.

Today there are a ton of brilliant designs to choose from. In comparison, this one's pretty basic. Even so it gets the job done just fine … and I'm terribly fond of it.

Most importantly, I'm comfortable with it. I know where everything's at without looking, and paint with it like it's a part of me. Ultimately, all of our equipment should become invisible to us while we paint—where stroke after stroke is laid down without a thought for our gear.

THE PANEL CARRIER

When the 9x12 pochade box was ordered, I added in a matching panel carrier as well. Identical in

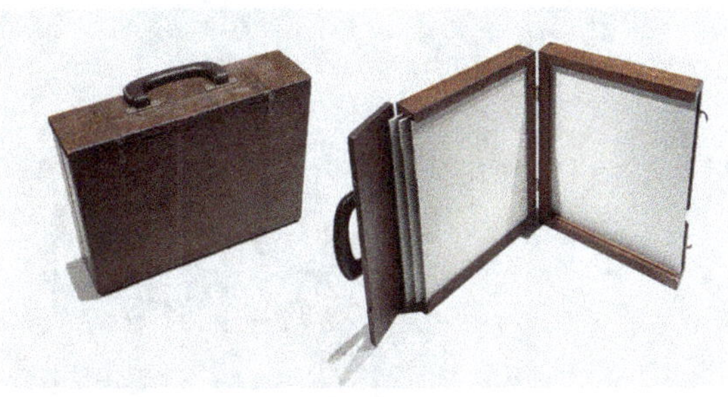

size, materials and shape—it's designed to carry six (wet or dry) canvas panels. Along with the two panels in the lid of my pochade box I could now bring along eight canvas panels at any given time. It added tremendous flexibility later on, where an entire day could be spent on location(s).

MY FRENCH EASEL

Occasionally I'd switch back and forth from the box to the French easel. The pochade box easily won out over time for small paintings. It's simply lighter and faster to set up. Sorolla had it right over 100 years ago; a pochade box really is the best solution when it comes to small field sketches.

That said, I LOVE my French easel and have zero regrets, other than the price I paid for it. It's fabulous for larger fieldwork—and has held up well over the decades.

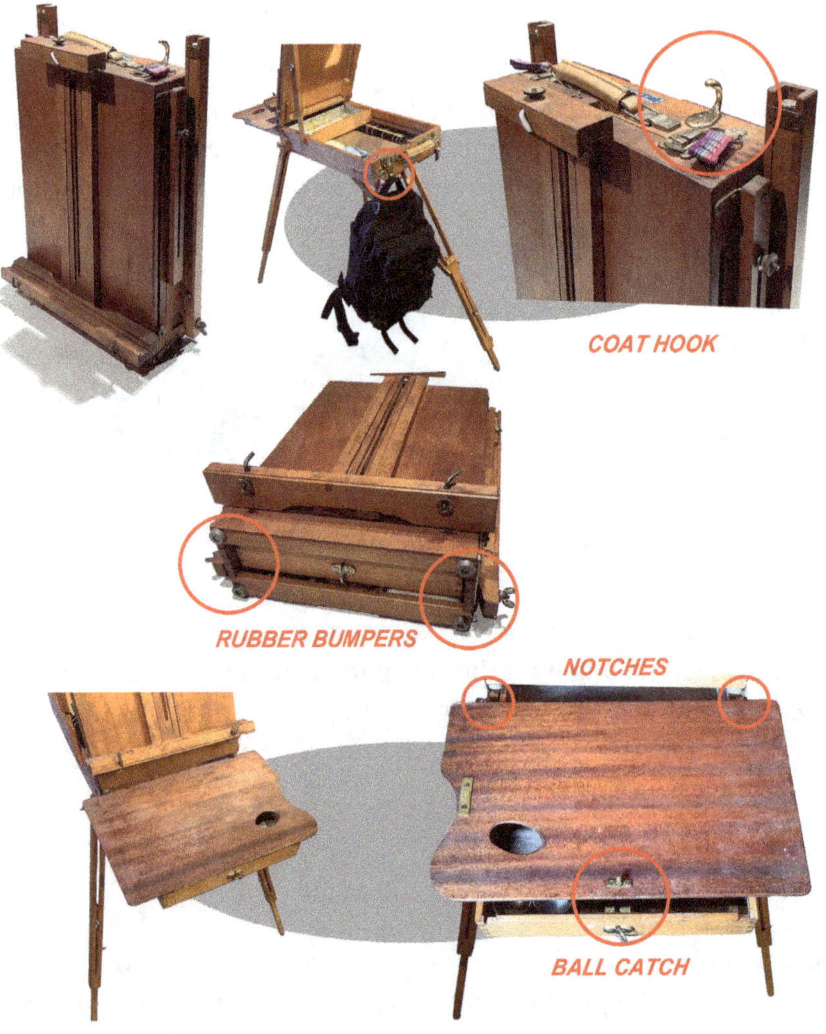

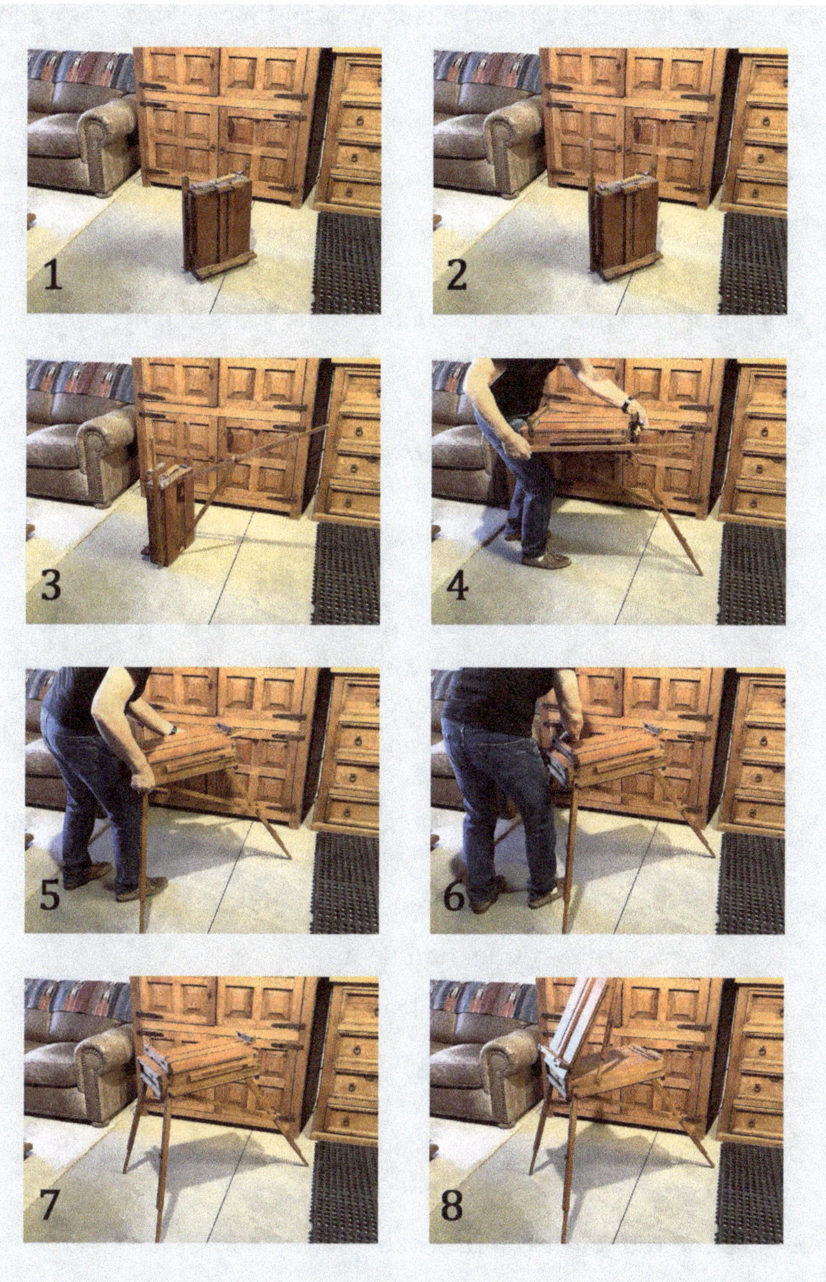

French Easel - Quick Set Up

If you've just bought a French easel, or plan to, here're a few minor additions to consider.

1. *Wipe wood-friendly oil over the entire exterior*—especially on and near the clamps that hold your canvas in place. I used Linseed oil. Though my easel came treated with something on it from the factory, its wood was still super porous. Oiling decreases the chances that wayward paint will become permanent additions.

2. *Add rubber bumpers to the bottom.* As the years slip by, you'll be glad you did. Home Depot or Lowe's usually has a selection on hand. (see illustration)

3. *Put a coat hook somewhere on the top.* Once the easel's up, it's remarkable just how much stuff you can hang on that dumb hook (back pack, coat, trash bag, etc.).

4. *Find something to attach the palette onto the drawer.* One friend of mine uses a large C-clamp to hold down his palette. Personally, I listened to a friend and notched the top edge of the wooden palette in two places and added a small two-piece *ball catch* onto the palette and drawer. Ball catches like this can be found online. I came across this one after a quick search - https://www.dlawlesshardware.com/solid-brass-double-ball-catch.html

Here are 8 steps to set up your French Easel quickly and efficiently:

1. Set it down on the ground, handle up

2. Extend the side legs upwards, leaving them attached to the easel

3. While still on the ground, fold out and extend the long center leg assembly

4. Lift the easel by the handle, rest its bottom end on your thigh and place the center leg on the ground

5. Swing out and lower the first extended side leg, then tighten the wing nut

6. Swing out and lower the second extended side leg and secure its wing nut

7. Set the easel on the ground

8. Lift the lid assembly, tighten the supports and you're ready to go!

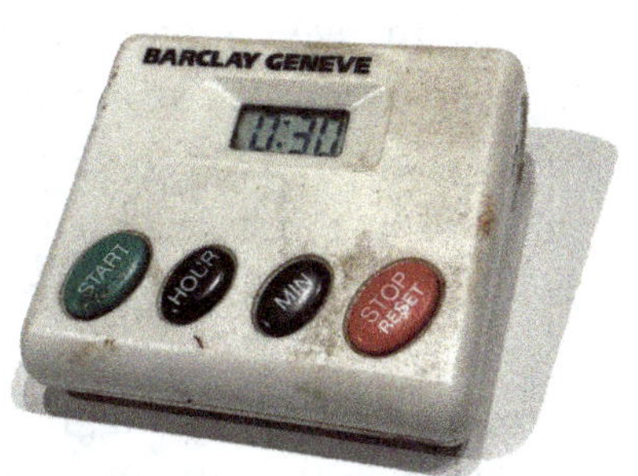

THE TIMER

Of course now we have timers on our mobile phones and iWatches … but they typically lack those critical 10 and 5-minute warnings.

Here's one of the small digital timers used to clock my half-hour sessions. We did a lot of paintings together.

You can still see my oily fingerprints on it. Timers like this have no mercy as workout partners.

UMBRELLA & RELATED GEAR

Here're a few benefits of using an umbrella:

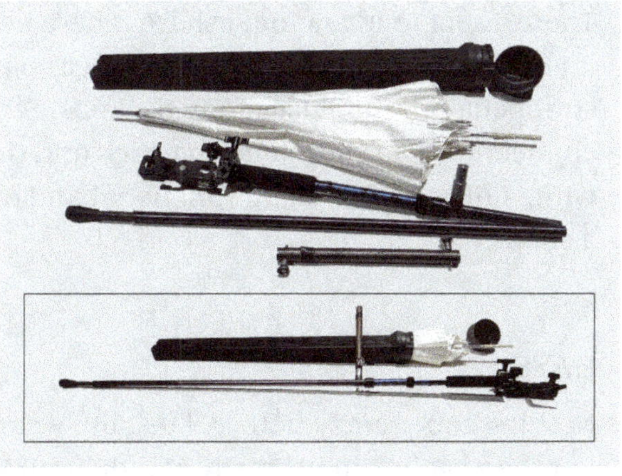

- The same uniform light illuminates both canvas and palette (critically important)
- On bright days it allows your pupils to dilate, letting in more color and light

- It reduces the effects of changing light overhead (intermittent clouds)
- It provides shade for the artist

I personally prefer using a white photographer's umbrella.
The clean, even light it offers is pretty spectacular to paint under.
Opaque umbrellas also work well; though normally provide cooler (bluer) light (800°K colder last time I measured). I won't get into the technical reasons behind that, other than to say it's largely due to the sky's blue canopy overhead.

After a bunch of testing, I finally designed the umbrella setup you'll see in the following illustration. I had it custom-made for me by a local outfit.

It uses a collapsible walking stick, shortened plastic case (originally designed for a construction level), tubular quick-release arm and corresponding mount located on the tripod's neck, articulating arm with mini-clamp and of course … a white umbrella.

There's a lot to it, and only share it here because I'd be remiss if I didn't. The umbrella (in its black case) and tripod are normally strapped onto the sides of my backpack, the removable tubular connecting arm slides into the pack and the walking stick is used while I hike. Lightweight, functional and everything sets up in a snap!

HATS

Nothing super-crazy here … I usually wear a baseball cap.
But then again, I'm normally standing under an umbrella. I think there's plenty of data already out there regarding the negative effects of sunlight on skin. Just consider wearing sunscreen and a good hat, you'll be glad you did.

One last thing … the time of day we paint absolutely affects
our UV exposure levels. The middle of the day, which I avoid for
artistic reasons, also delivers the greatest amount of UV damage.

TRIPOD

If you go with a
Pochade Box, you'll
need a good tripod.
I know, I know—
Joaquin Sorolla had
his sitting on his lap.
All I can say is: that was
then and this is now.
If Sorolla was around
today, he'd use a tripod
too.

Trying to paint like the
wind can be especially
tough if your Pochade
Box is wiggling around
due to a Mickey Mouse
tripod. So do yourself a
favor and get a good one.
I personally use a (now obsolete)
SLIK SH-705E Head sitting atop
SLIK PRO 330DX-B Legs.

It's getting along in years,
but still works great. Of course,
there are a zillion camera tripods
to choose from these days.

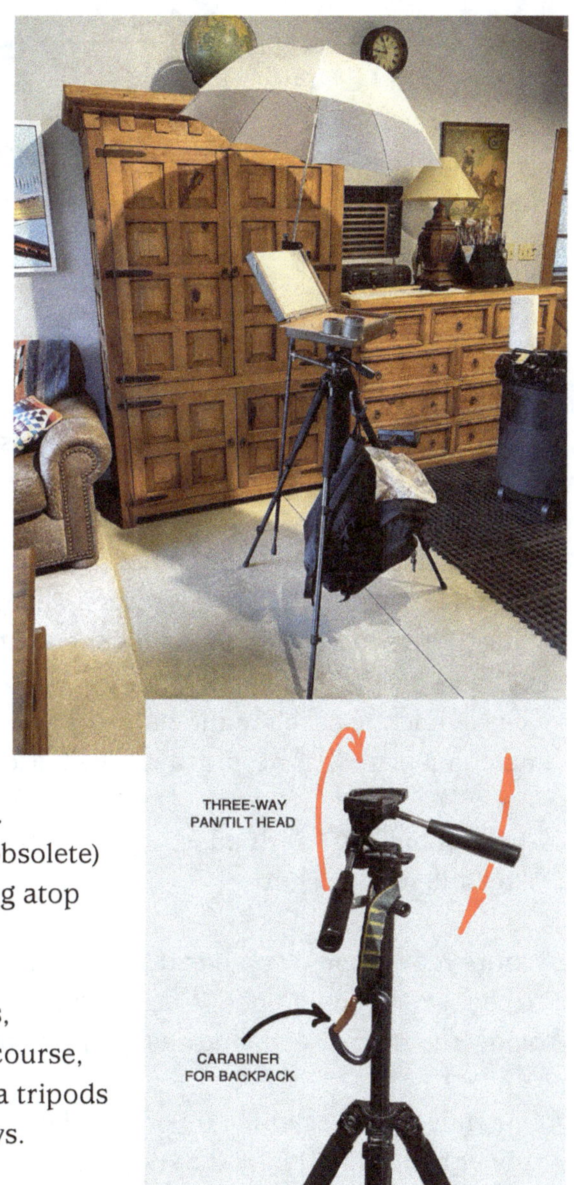

Virtually any modern tripod will work, as long as it's sturdy, and can lift your pochade box high enough where the top edge of your lid/canvas panel is roughly a foot below eye-level. (More on that later)

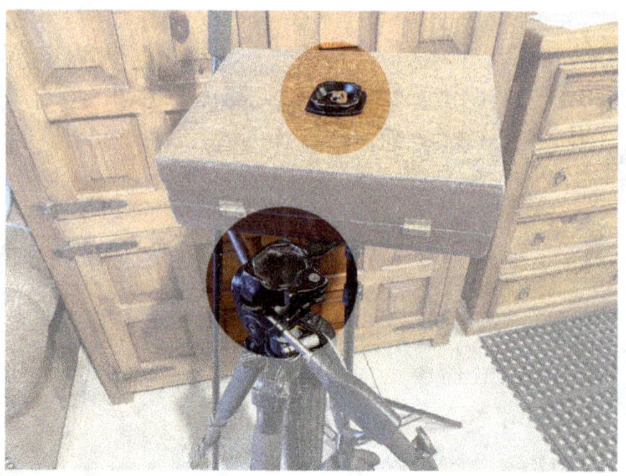

It should also have a *three-way pan/tilt head*. This allows for dynamic adjustment and quick leveling of your pochade box regardless of terrain.

You can also see a carabiner and strap assembly I use to secure the backpack onto the tripod while painting.

The ballistic nylon loop/handle located on the top of the backpack clips into the carabiner in moments. This allows the backpack to hang like a sandbag, adding greater stability to the entire setup.

I use a quick-release mount with my tripod. The SLIK head uses a matching plate that never leaves the bottom of my Pochade Box.

That's about it for a tripod: sturdy, three-way head, quick-release plate and not too short.

Before moving on, I should add the entire package (box, umbrella, tripod, etc.) is super light. When set up, it can all be grabbed just below the tripod head, and easily lifted and repositioned.

One time I set everything up on the shore, slipped on knee-high rubber boots, lifted it by the "neck" and carried it all out into the middle of a shallow stream. I found the spot I wanted, set it down in the water—and painted away, while the lower part of the tripod legs were underwater. When done, I grabbed it by the neck again, lifted it up and walked back to the shore. It worked like a charm ... only my boots and bottom sections of the tripod's legs ever got wet.

BRUSHES

This is where you should have some fun and experiment with various brushes until you find what you like.

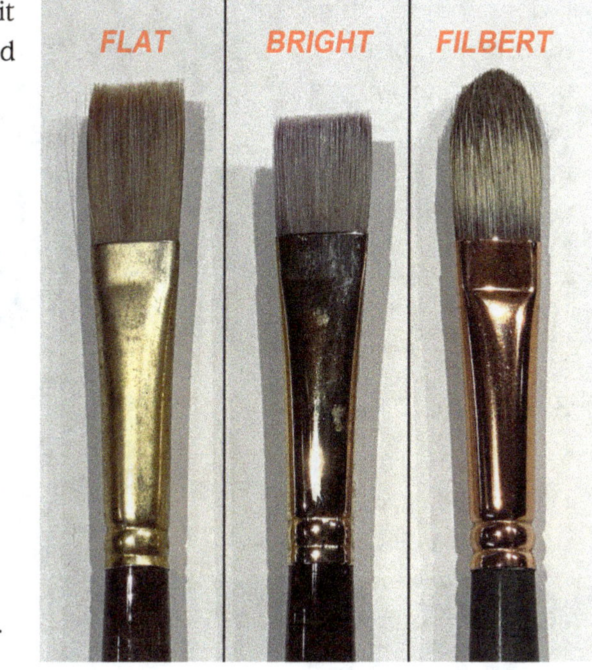

Here's a link to a 7-minute YouTube video on brush types I put together for absolute beginners – https://youtu.be/K8Fp0VWVees

I've personally used *Silver Grand Prix* hog-hair brushes outdoors for decades.

It's important to say here they're making some great synthetic brushes these days. That wasn't always the case. I particularly like the Princeton synthetics for studio work.

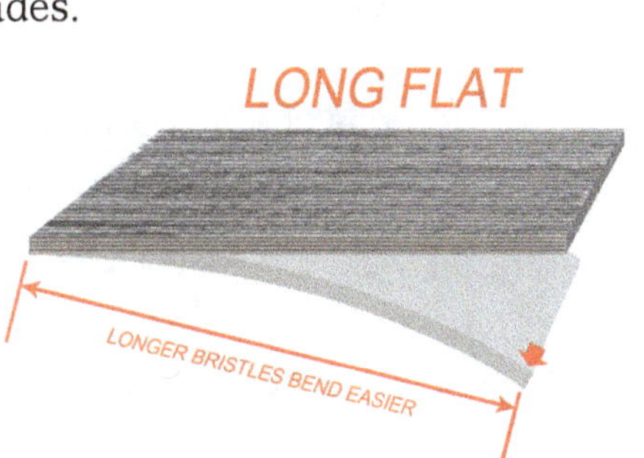

As I mention in my video, I almost always paint with *Brights*— indoors or out. I like their feel and the overall precision they provide. Their shorter bristles also help pick up more paint with the brush when I'm in a hurry.

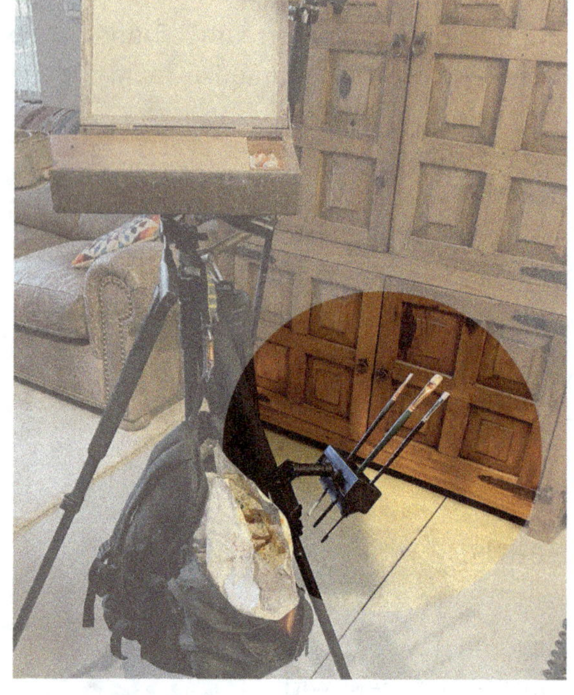

BRUSH HOLDER

Many years ago, I stumbled across this ingenious device. *I use it every day—in and out of the studio.* I've looked and looked, and never found anything quite like it.

It allows me to have 5 brushes out at one time ... and only one in my hand. The other four are firmly held by the *Brush Grip*—each waiting to be swapped out in a moment.

Made of some sort of tough black plastic, mine has held up incredibly well for *decades*. Honestly ... I don't see how I could get along without it.

The design has changed into something more compact and adaptive. I highly recommend getting one - https://www.easytouseproducts.com/product/brush-grip/.

THE LOWLY TURP CUP

I personally use the large, metal double-cup variety. One cup for turpentine to clean brushes, the other for medium (usually refined linseed oil).

I went for the larger cups because their mouths are easier to find with a brush when you're in a hurry. You're also less likely to run dry "mid-session."

A bit of serendipity: While assembling all my gear, I discovered the "guts" from a (then Japanese made) *Holbein Brush Cleaner No. 1A* would slide right into my large metal turp-cup.

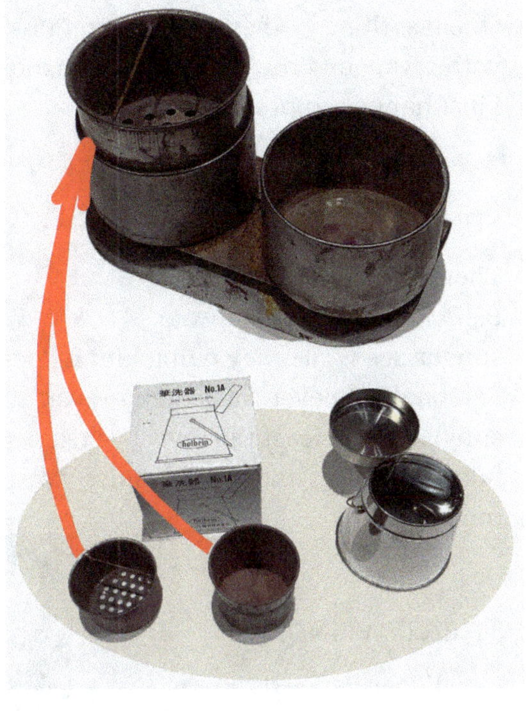

It makes a super compact, and efficient double-duty unit that clips right onto a palette.

NOTE: While writing this section, I became curious and looked to see if the same Holbein brush cleaner was still available after all these years. I actually found one … online with the same name. Though it looks similar, I suspect—like a lot of stuff these days—it's now made in China. As a result it may not fit quite the same as mine. If someone reading this happens to give a newer one a try, please let me know how it works.

One last thing … they make Turp Cups today (solvent/medium cups) with screw-on lids. They look fantastic, and probably work great. I just happen to prefer mine.

SUNGLASSES

There are some fabulous Plein Air painters that wear sunglasses while they paint, and it doesn't seem to hurt their work. Personally, I never wear them—ever. While painting outdoors, sunglasses (at least the ones I've tried) always seem to shift nuanced colors and subtle values way too much for my tastes. Just my two cents …

THE VIEWFINDER

Like Edgar Payne, I too recommend using a viewfinder, especially at the beginning.

It's easy to become overwhelmed by the amount of visual info we're supposed to cram onto a small canvas.

The viewfinder helps fix that. It quickly narrows down the area of focus, by creating finite boundaries for us.

I started out with a small cardboard version (shown), but soon found I needed something a little bit different.

Here's why: I'd hold up my cardboard viewfinder, look through it, find a paintable scene … then put it away. Once away, I'd quickly forget exactly where the boundaries were for the scene. So, I'd stop painting and hurry to pull it back out again for another look—again and again.

I decided I needed a fixed window of sorts … to look through *while* painting. Something always there to define—*and keep defining*— what I was scrambling to paint.

After some experimenting, I finally came up with a simple foldable gadget (shown below) and fastened it onto the lid of that first pochade box. It took seconds to raise and lower … and kept me locked on target during those initial months.

Of course, there's no rearranging of compositional elements with this setup, but I didn't care—not at this stage. I was busy juggling a zillion things during those 30minutes … and needed hardware that would help simplify and streamline the process. The "move things around stuff" could come later.

Here it is below: It was made from a wire coat hanger bent into a rectangle the same size as the canvas panel squarely beneath it.

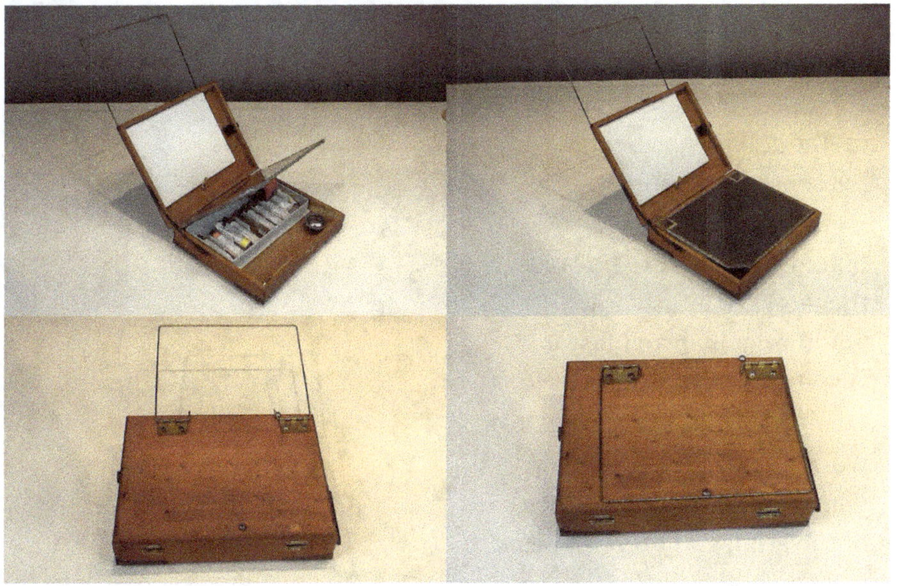

It passes through two hinge halves mounted onto the lid and clicks over two different screw heads that hold it up or keep it down.

Just like a set of training wheels on a bicycle needed at the beginning, I stopped using it when I switched boxes to my 9x12.

The only problem with using a fixed viewfinder (like the one below) is the need to close one eye each time you line up your scene. Each eye gives a slightly different view … so you need to pick an eye and stick with it. Looking back, I probably resembled a sort of "Plein Air Popeye" … one eye closed half the time while trying to figure out how to paint outdoors.

The following illustration shows it up on a tripod—with us looking through it. The surrounding landscape's colors have been muted to highlight the selected area.

Painting from life is largely a memory exercise on some level. Look, paint, look again, paint again, etc. So it only makes sense to shorten the time between looking and painting by placing your canvas edge next to your subject. This classic sight-size methodology has been used for centuries.

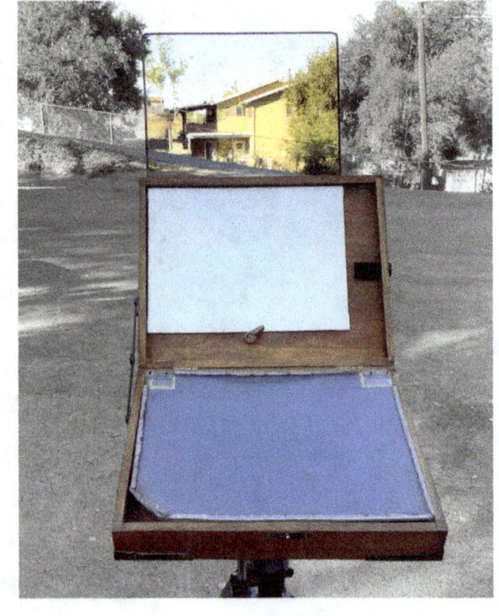

I mention that here because the viewfinder as shown automatically provides sight-size formatting. Classically trained this way for portrait work, I use this approach whenever I paint—in or out of the studio. My references, whether from photos or life, are either centered directly above, or beside my canvas. Now you can see the reason why I suggested your tripod be able to position your canvas to just below eye-level.

For those wondering, the hinged palette on this first box is clear Plexiglas with its underside covered with a middle value grey. Per Alex's advice, all the brushes used with this box had their handles shortened to fit into the small space near the paint tubes. Later on, when I shifted to the larger 9x12 pochade box (shown earlier) I began bringing my brushes along in a tubular carrier (shown later) allowing their handles to remain uncut.

Like so many things we aim ourselves at … in time, I improved. These days I still use a viewfinder, but mentally set the perimeter using fixed features in the landscape. For example: this bush is on the right-side boundary,

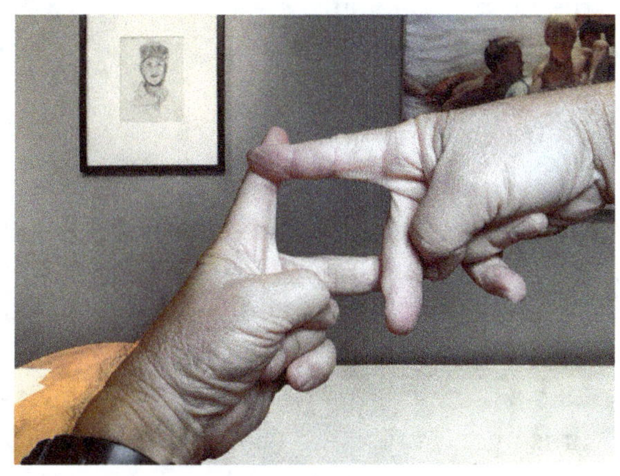

that tree trunk over there's on the left edge, etc. Which has allowed me to use the best viewfinder of all. It's remarkably lightweight and super easy to use …

PLASTIC SQUEEZE BOTTLES

Lightweight and nearly indestructible, I've used them for years to carry various art related liquids in my backpack—without

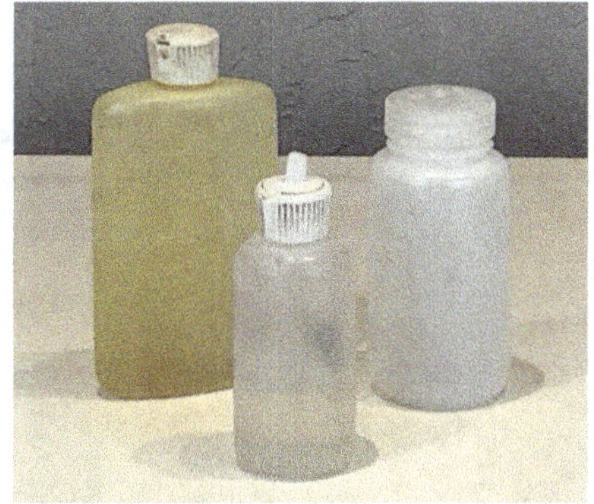

issue. The two on the left are pretty old … the new one on the right was recently picked up at a local outfitter.

Consider checking with the manufacturer of whatever bottles you choose, to make sure the liquids you plan to use are compatible.

BRUSH CARRIER

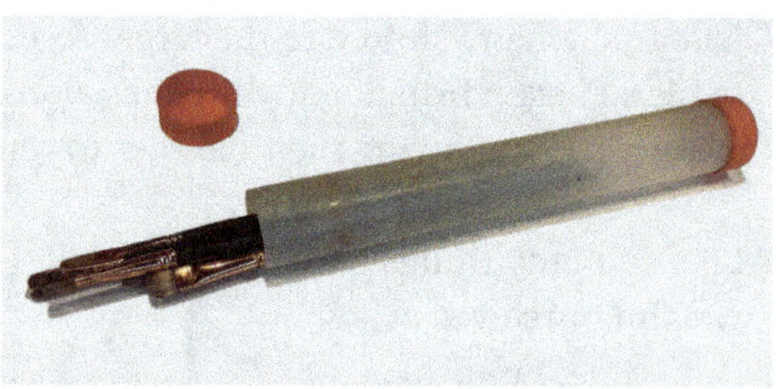

To avoid arriving at your location with the bristles on your brushes thrashed, keep them in a brush carrier during transport.

The two carriers I use aren't anything fancy—but they work great. The bottom line is, take a few simple precautionary steps to protect your brushes while traveling—you'll be glad you did.

Like a bunch of my gear, this first one was purchased a loooong time ago. It's become yellowed from use and old age, but still works fine. If using a backpack, slip this style into your pack vertically—with the brush tips pointing upwards.

The brush holder below works well with a French easel. It rolls the brushes up together and then slips nicely into the lower storage section. If you keep your brush ends away from the carrier's edge while rolling it up (tightly), it won't matter if the tips are pointing up or down.

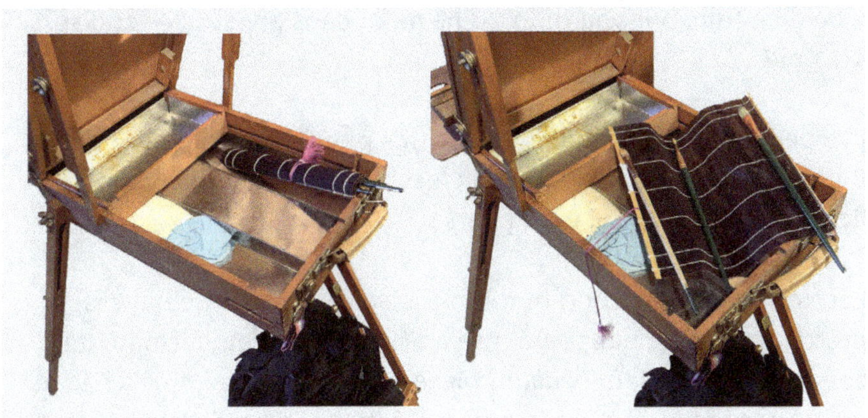

THE MULTI-TOOL

You've just arrived somewhere gorgeous. The sun's just starting to set and everything looks INCREDIBLE! You can hardly wait to start painting!!

You hurry, setting up your painting gear in record time. Then try to squeeze some paint onto your palette, and find the small twist-on caps are stuck solid on a couple tubes! It's like they're welded on! No matter how hard you try, they won't budge. OH-NO!

So there you are, standing smack dab in the middle of Plein Air paradise, with no way to get your paint caps off. What now?

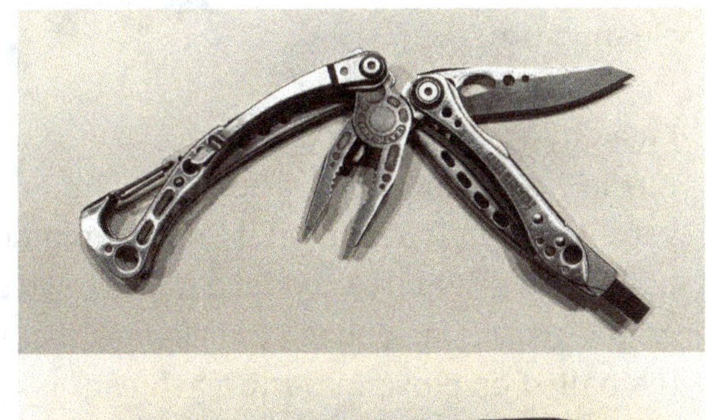

Well, if you'd thought to bring along a small pair of pliers, everything

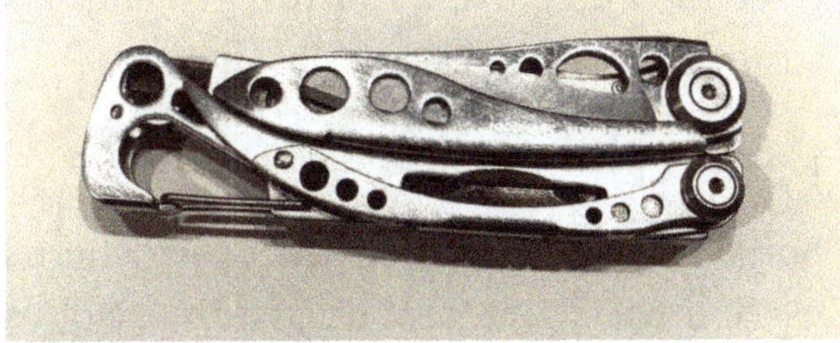

would be fine, but you didn't. The paint caps are stuck—and so are you!

I've personally lived that scenario. It's painful when it happens. But then pain can be a fabulous teacher. My solution became a lightweight multi-tool with pliers.

I gotta say, the selection of multi-tools available these days is pretty amazing. I happen to use a *Skeletool* by Leatherman. It's a compact, lightweight *brilliant* piece of engineering. Mine's had a ton of hard miles put on it, and still functions flawlessly.

GLOVES

There are some that don't "feel like they're an artist" if they wear gloves while painting. Not me … I'm much too practical. They can radically reduce field cleanup time.

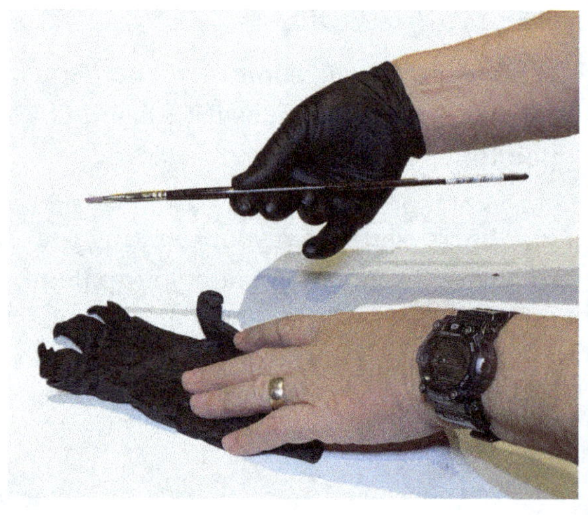

I usually wear the nitrile 7mil disposable variety. The 7mil thickness is rugged and yet thin enough to slip on without too much effort. When I'm done painting, I grab any wayward paper towels that might've ended up on the ground, peel back the glove while holding them and toss the balled up glove into my trash bag.

FOOTWEAR

Some people wear sneakers everywhere they go, including outdoors to paint, and do just fine. Not me, I'm flatfooted. So in

my case, what goes on my feet while I stand to paint matters
A LOT!

There's a long story (that I won't get into), where I'd hiked in
a ways to paint—wearing cheap boots. No kidding, the next
morning it felt like somebody had taken a baseball bat and beat
the bottoms of my feet. MAN, they hurt!

About a week later … after I was able to walk a little better, I went
to a local outfitter and bought some (really expensive) hiking
boots. They're scary comfortable, have *incredible* support and
make my flat feet feel downright bulletproof.

I've traveled overseas to paint, hiked up in the Eastern Sierras
(with my painting gear) in those boots, and my feet have never felt
thrashed like that again. If you're like me, spend the money and
get some decent boots. Your feet will thank you later.

LEGGINGS/POLAINAS

Before I get into this, I should confess that I almost never wear
them. They're a complete pain to put on and take off. Ninety-nine
percent of the time they're excessive, even useless. BUT! There *are*
times and places I've painted where they're a priceless addition
to my legs.

I actually own two pairs. One set's made of black, ballistic nylon
with super long Velcro closures right up the front. They're perfect
for hiking through deep snow or thick brush. I've hiked through
2-3 feet of fresh snow up near Mammoth to paint, and was thrilled
to have them on.

Then there's the leather pair …
Years ago, a friend told me how he'd been out Plein Air painting in

the backcountry several days earlier. It was one of those gorgeous, sunny days that San Diego's famous for.

Excited to get at it, he quickly set up his French Easel and immediately dove into painting. After some serious, non-stop effort, he finally took a breather and stepped back to get a better look at his painting. That's when he happened to notice a HUGE diamondback rattler quietly napping under his easel in the shade —about two feet from where he'd been standing.

After a minute … he managed to calm down enough to run the rattlesnake off. Phew! When I heard that story, I thought—that could've been me!

A little research revealed most snakebites occur below the kneecap.

So, I had a local saddle-shop make a pair of leggings from nice thick leather.

They're called Polainas (pō-lī'-năhz) in Spanish. Mexicans have worn them forever.

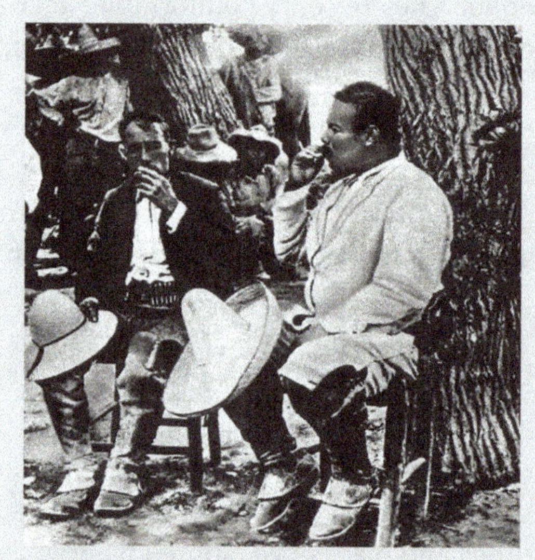

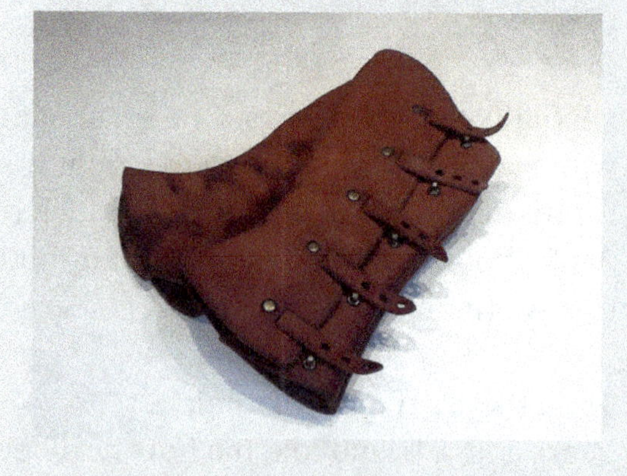

Here's a shot of Pancho Villa wearing his (taller) Polainas.

I gotta say, they're really pretty amazing—like having "leg-armor" on.

They're easily overkill—that is unless I happen to accidently step on a rattlesnake, or bump against some cactus out in the middle of nowhere!

THE BAREBONES GEAR CHECKLIST:
(Just tell me the minimum I need to get started!)

- Outdoor Easel or Pochade Box (w/tripod)
- Brushes
- Oil Paints - Professional Grade
- 8x10 or 9x12 Canvas Panel(s)
- Medium/Turpentine Cups
- Turpentine (or substitute - in a jar or bottle)
- Backpack or Bag (to carry everything in)
- Roll of paper towels
- Disposable Plastic Bag (for used paper towels)
- Timer (or Android/iPhone w/timer app)
- Viewfinder
- Pliers or Multi-tool

The other items discussed, that are not on this list aren't critical. Aside from the last two items (pliers and viewfinder), this is exactly what I started out with.

I'd suggest you begin with the essentials, and see how you do. It's easy to spend your cash on more gear later on.

I'll close this section on equipment with some advice … advice I wish somebody'd told me before my first time out.

Test-drive everything before you're out in the field. Practice some "dry runs" beforehand—someplace convenient, like in your back yard. Wherever. I didn't, I just went for it on location, and immediately regretted it. Be smarter than I was, and become acquainted with your entire setup beforehand. LIVE the process while you're not under pressure.

While at home, pack it all up, just as if you're going to travel with it. Then unpack it like you're standing out in a field somewhere. Get everything set up, maybe even paint a small 30-minute "practice sketch" of something … anything. You can always wipe down your practice sketch panel with turp and reuse it. Clean up and pack it all back up again … a few times over several days. You'll grow your understanding of the process, uncover any weaknesses in your gear and gain confidence before "making the jump to light speed".

Notes

Notes

CHAPTER 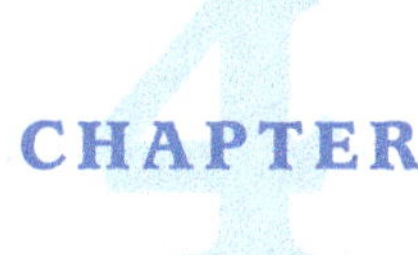

Take The Leap!

After those practice sessions at home, go over the bullet points that follow, then head out and paint your first piece *on location* before reading much further.

Your first attempt in the field will help you gain some gritty understanding that'll help to fashion a schedule for yourself.

Here are some suggestions for the first few times out on location (also stuff I wish someone had told me beforehand)

- Consider keeping a larger journal or notebook for the lessons learned.

- If it's sunny, try to start your painting session before 10:00am or after 3:00pm (more on that later).

- Pick somewhere convenient and comfortable ... close to home if you can.

- Try to find someplace absent bystanders. People are naturally curious about outdoor painters. They mean no harm, but can be an enormous distraction, especially when you're just starting out.

- Avoid gusty winds—even the best struggle to paint in high winds.

- Find a scene that's uncomplicated ... something with large, simple patterns of light and shadow.

- Paint a scene that's not too distant, with the farthest point under 100yards away.

- *It's okay to fail!* I sure did—A LOT! (more on that later)

- Think about putting something down in your vehicle for your painting gear to rest on while traveling—an old towel, anything. Wet paint can end up in places on your gear that you don't notice until you're back home, and it's too late.

- Make sure your hands don't have paint on them before grabbing the steering wheel to drive home. How do you suppose I know that?! Again, disposable gloves are an easy fix.

- Keep your "field cleanup" time to a minimum. Purpose to do just enough to get you all packed up and back home. Thorough cleanup is *always* faster and more efficient at home.

THE SCHEDULE

My own was pretty aggressive right from the start. Monday-Friday, I set aside an hour to do a small painting on location after work and then head home. It was roughly 15minutes to park and set up the painting gear, 30minutes of painting *(furiously)* … then another fifteen to pack up and climb back in the car.

Of course the schedule was always open to "adjustment". Count on things cropping up that you'll have to adapt to like time changes, rain, family obligations, etc.

Step 3

Get in shape for the trip

It probably goes without saying that these high-pressure, 30-minute painting exercises were designed to get me in shape—and they did! They were hard-core, artistic fitness training that helped turn me into a pro.

TRY NOT TO MISS A WORKOUT

If I somehow missed a weekday workout, which I did at times, I'd try to make it up on Saturday. I hated missing a day. It always felt like I'd cheated myself.

WHICH BRINGS ME TO: FAILURE IS PART OF THE PROCESS!

I think it's important to say pushing for noticeable gains in nearly anything just about guarantees we're going to experience short-term defeat.

It's easy to forget toddlers fall countless times before walking. The truth is: *Failure's not a roadblock to success—when used properly, it's a fast lane to it!*

To quote Thomas J. Watson (IBM's legendary chairman/CEO) - *"If you want to increase your success, double your failure rate!"*

Step 4

Make the exercises harder than the actual trip

To be doubly clear, right from the start this timed outdoor painting stuff was meant as a way to rapidly improve me and my studio paintings—period. My goal, the ultimate destination (Step 1) ... was to do whatever it took to start advancing again and ultimately turn professional. I was prepared to work hard at it. It shouldn't come as a surprise when I say after several months of torturous half hour workouts; regular studio painting began to feel downright easy.

If we begin treasuring every outdoor workout sketch we produce, we're probably doomed from the start.

Here's why, we're in danger of caring way too much about each and every brush stroke we make ... while trying to throw caution to the wind? Sure. Fear usually wins out in a scenario like that. I know. Timidity can and will short-circuit the daring attitude we're trying to foster. We're out to push the envelope … to stretch our unseen, fear-limiting boundaries. That only happens through repeated risk-taking in the proper environment and structure.

Here's the deal … at its core, we're trying to beat the fear of failure into submission *by learning to look at our failures differently.* We want a system of practice in place, where failing (gradually) becomes okay—*because YOU are the ultimate product, not the painting.* If you crank out a loser, so what! Big Deal! Learn from it, throw it away (more on that in Chapter 5) and go at it again tomorrow. Like Walt Disney used to say: *Keep moving forward!* As you stick with it and improve (and you will), so will every painting that follows—because you've become a better artist.

WHEN ALL THE PLANETS ALIGN

I want to pause here in the middle of all this "failure is okay" stuff to say, this really does work. I promise that if you apply yourself, things do get better. In fact, it's quite breathtaking when it starts to happen. It sure was for me. Small brilliant victories suddenly began showing up in the middle of my otherwise failure-ridden week.

There were even days where complete perfection just seemed to show up out of nowhere! I'm not sure I have the words to describe it, but it was as if I wasn't the one standing there doing the painting! As if I'd become a sort of bystander, watching the sketch paint itself—right before my eyes. Bizarre.

I've repeatedly experienced this phenomenon. It's pretty mind-bending whenever it happens. Everything's suddenly sublime, and works … perfectly.

BREAKTHROUGHS

While on the subject of ups and downs, it might be good for you to hear I'd also experience strings of brutally frustrating days. Mini-plateaus, if you will. In spite of that, I'd doggedly stick with it, and then suddenly I'd slam out another winner. Just good old persistence paying off over time! Again and again, if I were diligent, I'd experience repeated breakthroughs.

Here's the fun part, there were elements within these breakthrough sketches that *I couldn't have done the week before.*

Don't be surprised when important gains show up on the heels of a discouraging dry spell. The secret is DON'T GIVE UP!

I've managed to hang onto a few of what I personally consider landmark or next-level paintings (for me) from back then. They're not great pieces of art, just indicators at the time, that I was making progress. I have one hanging in my studio right now … a constant reminder of how things can and do get better— if we'll only stick with it.

Notes

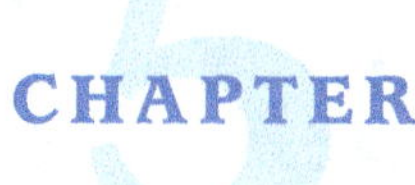

CHAPTER

Progress, Practicalities & Adaptations

*Continuous improvement is better
than delayed perfection*

– MARK TWAIN –

PROGRESS

As the months passed, the *unexpected benefits* listed earlier
began to appear. Bolder brushwork became commonplace,
my routine—became, well, routine. My confidence as a painter
grew exponentially, and the work showed it.

It just wasn't a big deal anymore to do a painting. How could it be?
I was creating a brand new piece almost every day.

Step 5

*Increase your failure rate during the exercises
—stretch yourself*

The road to victory will be strewn with the wreckage of
our countless failures.

FRISBEE ART

As mentioned earlier, I'd learn what I could from each sketch,
then throw it away if I didn't like it—which happened a lot.
**The act of learning and improving was far more important than
the painting itself.**

Not sure why it took so long for me to fully understand that
deeper truth. I mean, DUH! It's why I'd started out doing all this
in the first place. Sacrifice everything else to produce a superior
artist—me! It became crystal clear that every outdoor sketch was
merely a stepping-stone towards my larger goal.

I'd keep the good ones and trash the rest—no mercy.

I'd been using inexpensive canvas panels all along—the one
place I'd fudged on buying the very best (sorry Alex). They were
made of rugged cotton canvas and at the time ran about 30¢/ea.
The low price made it easier to rationalize chucking one.
Though inexpensive, I gotta say they were remarkably well
made back then. Decades later, the surviving sketches done on
those panels are holding up just fine.

Speaking of the rejects … after awhile, I affectionately began referring to them as "Frisbees", because they flew just about like a Frisbee on final approach to the trashcan. Over time, I got pretty good at putting just the right spin on a small panel while throwing it.

CANVAS TOOTH

I soon discovered the lifespan of my (expensive) brushes was *directly* tied to how much "tooth" the small canvas panels had on them. Whether we realize it or not, the tips of our brushes slowly disappear with every stroke we make.

Obviously, sharper canvas tooth wears out brushes faster. (Coarse canvas = shorter brush life, smooth canvas = longer brush life.) This became especially apparent after I began painting almost every day. No kidding, I could literally watch my brushes grow shorter by the week. I had to do something.

Here are two Silver Brush Ltd. *Grand Prix* Brights shown side by side—one used, the other new. You can readily see the effects canvas

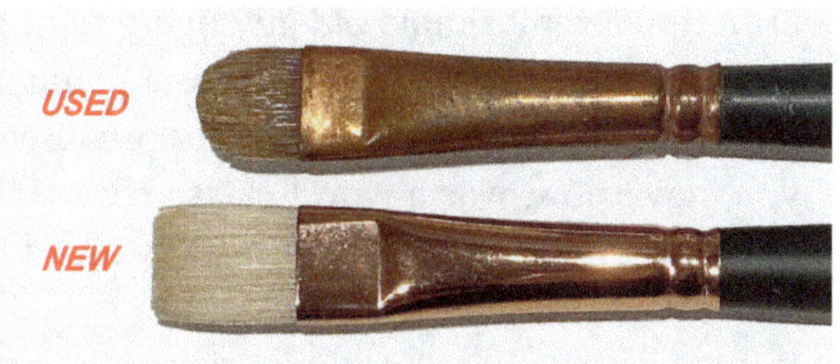

tooth has had on the upper brush. My cheap panels were eating up my pricey brushes—fast!

Because I wanted to keep using my "financially friendly" panels— I began reducing their tooth a bit. After some experimenting, I finally settled on making long passes over the canvas' face with a one-sided razorblade, holding it at 90° to the panel's surface. (See photos)

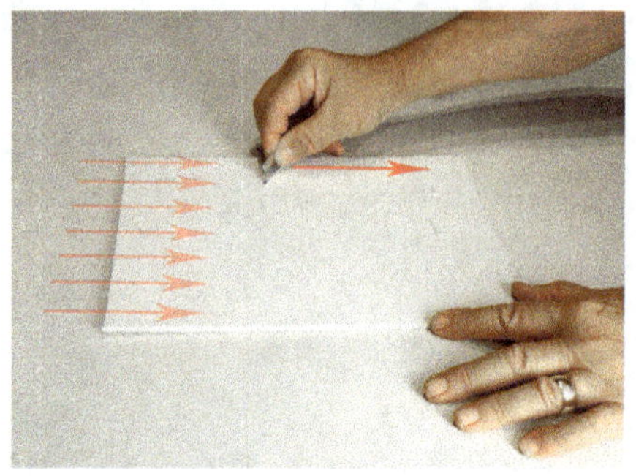 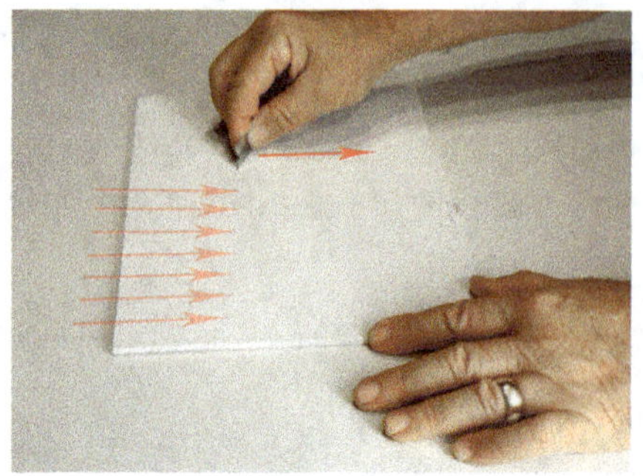

I'd scrape the entire primed surface, in two different directions—first long ways, then side-to-side—until the panel began feeling a bit smoother. By the way, if you happen to do this, be careful not to remove too much gesso. Leave enough primer for your paint to grab onto.

SIZE MATTERS
(keep your paintings small outside)

While on the subject of canvas … not long after all this began I ran into a remarkable old guy living right here in San Diego. His name was Darwin Duncan. As a young man, he'd actually painted with Edgar Payne up in Laguna Beach. Payne, as some of you may know, was a world-class artist, leader within the Early California Impressionist community and a *brilliant author*.

While visiting with Darwin in his studio, he casually mentioned that Payne almost never worked larger than 12x16 outdoors. He said Payne would work small on location, then take his diminutive sketches back to the studio where he'd use them to create larger works.

Hearing Edgar Payne had painted small and fast outdoors was fabulous information for me at the time. It virtually paralleled what I was already doing.

To this day, there are times I'll do a small, quick oil study on location for a project I'm doing—even a figurative scene. It helps me gather much better information than a camera could ever provide. Then, like Payne, these small sketches are used as a wonderful reference back in the studio.

While on the subject of Mr. Payne, I *highly* recommend getting your hands on his landmark book, *Composition of Outdoor Painting*. Out of print for years, it's thankfully become available 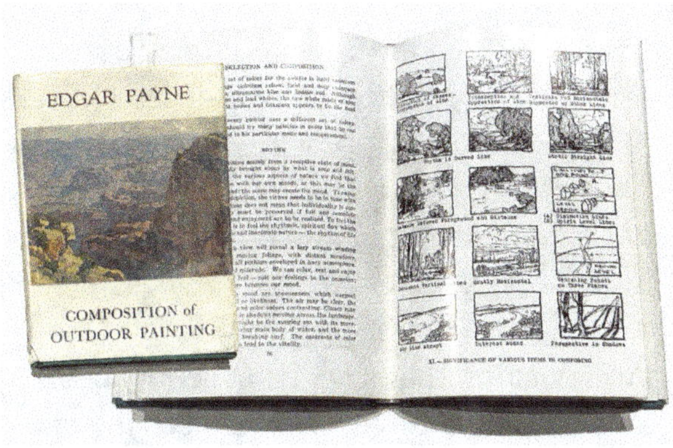 once again. It has insights into painting and composition that continues to influence my own professional work.

Step 6

See yourself where you want to go, and how it'll feel when you get there

I've purposely put this step directly after Edgar Payne's book. All the research, the zillions of paintings, the countless trips to museums to see plein air masterpieces done by the likes of Payne made a deep impression on me. It helped me to "see" in my imagination, what it would look like to eventually pull it all off.

THE CREATIVE SHIFT

Remember my account of the first time out—where I heard the timer's ten-minute warning, and I suddenly began to paint faster? THEN the five-minute warning ... where even greater risks and wild-eyed painting took place?

EVERYTHING got thrown out in a supreme effort to cover that tiny canvas with paint before the dumb clock ran out. Then suddenly—BEEEEEP!!! Time's up?!!!

I felt ... exasperated and beat up ... which was, of course, intentional.

I'm revisiting that important sequence here, because the timer and its maddening warnings near the end *relentlessly* pushed me toward an imaginary cliff. Those remaining fear-filled moments somehow shifted me, as if by magic, out of my logical un-artistic *left*-brain—and into my intuitive/wonderfully artistic *right*-brain.

For those that've never heard of Dr. Roger Sperry, allow me to introduce him. In 1981 Sperry was awarded the Nobel Prize for his groundbreaking scientific discoveries revealing the differing functionalities between the right and left hemispheres of the human brain. For those new to Sperry's work, I'll oversimplify here and cut to the chase. Sperry determined that we read/speak etc. from our logical left hemisphere and imagine/create (and paint our best) from our right hemisphere.

As it turned out, those frantic final few minutes of painting were shifting me into an unforeseen neurological, artistic experience. I had to completely abandon what I thought I knew technically, and begin trusting my "other self". That's the only way I can describe it. Tom's process had unearthed a hidden part of me that was remarkably intuitive and better at painting. The act of painting suddenly became wonderfully different ... something bigger.

Interestingly, as time passed it appeared that repeated 30-minute sessions were actually fostering more of these creative shifts. They weren't just happening outdoors. They began to show up in the studio as well. My guess is that accessing this neurological door again and again had somehow eased its opening.

I'll add this new "going right brain" behavior, began making things less ... predictable. For example, around this time my wife unexpectedly walked into my studio (unannounced) while I was painting away and asked me a simple question. Right then I was deeply immersed in my new Right-Brain-Creative-Mode. Inwardly, I was a zillion miles away when she began talking to me.

I somehow heard her question, turned around to answer—*and found I couldn't speak!* It was *really* weird at the time! After several moments something changed and I could suddenly talk. I wasn't quite sure what had happened. Years later I shared the strange incident with a neurosurgeon I met, before I'd heard of Sperry. He smiled knowingly and said, "Chris, that was perfectly normal— you're fine". He then went on to describe in perfect detail the neurological shift we've been covering.

Because of that event (and others like it), today, if we're driving through say, a scenic area, my wife will usually ask to take the wheel ... so I can slip unchecked into my right-brain/artistically creative mode..

MUSCLE MEMORY

Something else I discovered worth mentioning here is—muscle memory. It pertains to repetitive actions we (eventually) do without consciously thinking about it. Everyone's done stuff on "autopilot". We button our shirt or tie our shoes without overtly thinking about it. Even complex activities like driving a car can become largely automatic over time. Though termed Muscle Memory, it really has more to do with the neural connections formed from repetitive behaviors.

There's actually been loads of research done on the subject. We learn something, and over time it requires less (and less) focused attention.

The same adaptive process applies to painting. Where we put our brushes, our layout of colors across the palette, where we place the turpentine or medium cup, etc. can become terribly important. It all matters … especially after using it for a while.

The painting process, like driving a car, quickly becomes highly automated. Some years ago, I had occasion to paint in a friend's (massive/gorgeous/professional) studio. I was surprised to find it unbelievably hard to paint there! It was like trying to cook in someone else's kitchen—everything was in the wrong place. Each action I took, both large and small, demanded (slower) conscious thought.

So do yourself a favor and keep your key painting elements organized into a regular, repeatable system. Again, where you place your brushes, your medium, your paper towels or rags, how you arrange your paints on your palette, etc. You can move stuff around for a while until you find out what works best for you. BUT once you decide what that ideal placement system is, I strongly advise you avoid moving things around after that. You want everything to be as automatic or habit-based as possible while you paint.

HABITS

Speaking of habits, I think we can all agree they can be incredibly powerful … and can either help or hurt us. So purpose to use them to your advantage during this process. Go beyond simply idealizing your painting layout. Make everything you can into a system—even the small stuff.

Figure out the best way to organize the gear in your backpack (if you use one), the most efficient method to clean up in the field—and at home. How to clean your palette each time that works the best, etc.

Setting up a French easel (shown in the earlier illustration) in a prescribed way is one example. It's a systemized and efficient approach on how we do something … again and again. I could grab my French easel right now, and quickly set it up the way it's shown, almost without thinking. I've done it that way so many times that it's become second nature.

Every one of us applies this to things in our life—purpose to do it with this too. I should add that if a better way to do a process shows up, as so often happens, use it instead. Constant improvement.

You'll discover that once you get a method in place that you're happy with, if you stick to it, it'll quickly become habit. Again, apply that mindset to as much as possible, and you'll be amazed at how easy things get after awhile. They'll simply add up. Though there's differing data out on this, one source stated it usually takes about 21 days for something to become a habit. So if you find a way that works, stick it out for about 3 weeks and there's a good chance it'll become just about automatic.

THE WEATHER

I'm sorry, I know—I'm spoiled living here in San Diego. What can I say? I was born here. But then Southern California's glorious weather is the reason things cost so much here … and why Edgar Payne and the gang came here to paint over a hundred years ago. So though I live in a plein air paradise, I completely understand harsh weather in other places can become an issue with a program like this.

I mention that because even though I live in San Diego, I *have* experienced a ton of rough conditions and bad weather firsthand while painting.

I've personally stood painting landscapes in the middle of High Sierra snow flurries, had my gear hurled against rocks from gusting winds near the ocean and painted in scorching 115+° heat in the Anza-Borrego Desert.

Years ago, I was painting all alone up in the Eastern Sierras. I happened to be in the middle of a gorgeous glacial lake/mountain scene when high-winds suddenly showed up. In moments, the lake's serene surface erupted into choppy whitecaps.

The change in the lake was okay; it was already painted in. But the mountains behind it weren't quite done … I needed just a *little* more time. So without pausing, I reached up, grabbed the umbrella's shaft to keep it from snapping off, and kept right on painting.

I guess my point is … like Winston Churchill so famously said: *"Keep Buggering on!"* Overcome, whenever and wherever possible, because problems WILL show up!

Depending on where you live, you'll certainly have legitimate reasons not to go paint that day. Yet, like so many things in life, it usually comes down to our own personal commitment. *Just how badly do we want to improve?* Only you can say, and each situation will, in its own way, be unique.

If you can't paint outside that day, why not set up a quick still life indoors instead? Time yourself and go for it inside. Just like the outdoors, keep your lighting simple on your still life—keep it down to one source if possible. *Sir Henry Raeburn's* portraits are stunning examples of what can be done under simple, single-source lighting indoors.

The point is, do <u>something</u>. Again, try not to miss whenever possible. Your sub-conscious, internal artist that you're trying to build will know each and every time you skip out on your routine.

Brilliant violinist Jascha Heifetz famously said: *The discipline of practice every day is essential. When I skip a day, I notice a difference in my playing. After two days, the critics notice, after three days, so does the audience.*

Like Jascha Heifetz, I too believe intuitive, muscle-memory dynamics are quietly lifted to new heights and maintained, through consistent effort.

THE TIME OF DAY

Beyond just trying to squeeze painting sessions into my (already) busy schedule, at the beginning I honestly had no idea that the time of day mattered. I found out quickly it does … A LOT!

Like a bunch of other outdoor activities, the optimal time of day can be affected by the weather. For example: A high overcast or

Sky Lit day provides the most stable and static light to paint under. Your shadows remain almost stationary. As long as both you and your scene stay under 100% cloud cover, the typical hard-edged shadows carved out by the sun won't exist.

That's because you, and everything else around you, are in one gigantic shadow while you paint.

The shadows we see on *Sky Lit* days are in reality penumbras … the darker shadow within a shadow. When you're painting under high overcast, you're basically working in one of those shadowed regions shown on the photo below.

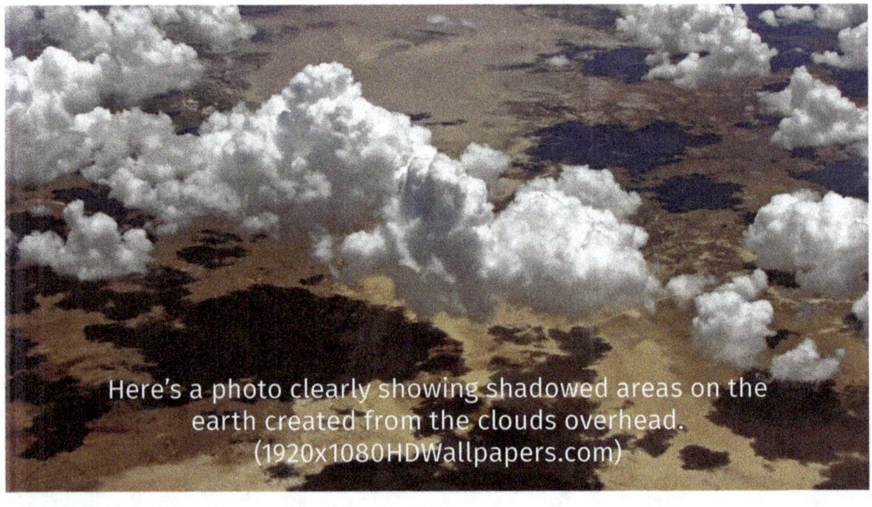

Conversely, painting outdoors during bright, *Sunlit* days will have you hustling to capture the moving shadow patterns that are zipping by at 15°/hr.

I smile and tell people that painting outdoors on a sunny day is like trying to paint someone walking slowly, because <u>everything's</u> moving!

Because the direct sunlight patterns are so fleeting, I always try to get them laid in first—and fast. Then leave them alone as they change. I've done it the other way, and invariably get mired down chasing shadows until the last brush stroke. Bad idea.

PENUMBRA VS. CAST SHADOWS

To further clarify, here's an illustration with two figures (courtesy John Asaro) shown side by side. The figure to the left was shot using a white photo diffuser fitted onto a studio lamp.

The lighting effect created by the diffuser is almost identical to

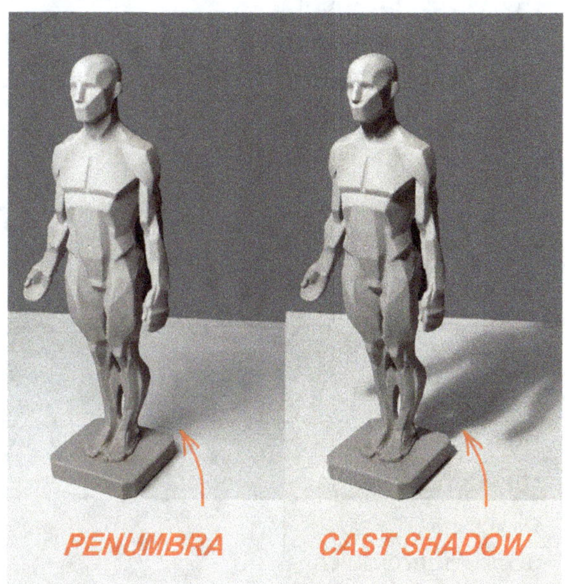

overhead cloud cover outdoors. The clouds act like a huge diffuser between the sun and us. Though it may not look like it … the left figure is actually standing in relative shadow—with only the *Penumbra,* or *shadow within the shadow* evident on the ground behind it.

In contrast, the figure on the right was illuminated without a filter … just harsh, unchecked light. This mirrors the effect of direct sunlight typically found on a bright clear day. The shadows appear hard and dark in comparison, with clearly defined edges.

In summary: the shadows we see produced during high, overcast days are really soft penumbras and incredibly stable … conversely, shadows created by direct sunlight are hard, dark and move—fast.

DIRECTIONAL SUNLIGHT

It's important to understand the angle that direct sunlight strikes your location has a HUGE effect on the scene before you.

Due to its high inclination, noonday sunlight creates minimal shadow patterns, tending to flatten everything out. It also cuts through a lot less of the earth's atmosphere on the way to you. This produces super clean and less chromatic light.

On the other hand, low, early morning or late afternoon sunlight slices through a ton of the earth's atmosphere. This causes it to become wonderfully chromatic, before forming those long

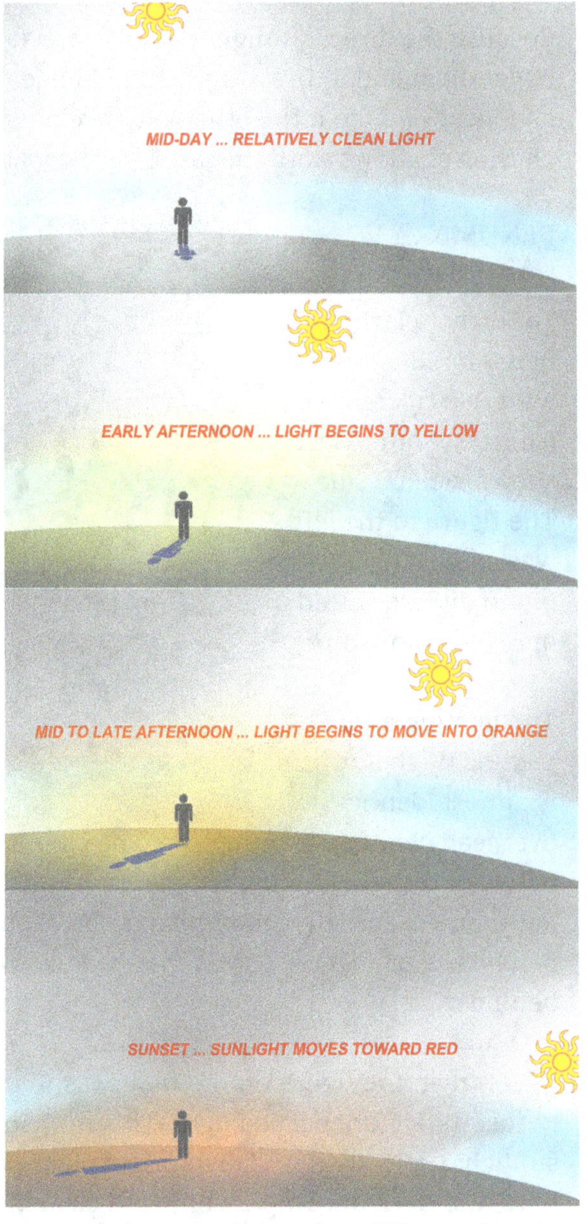

Here I've created a series of illustrations approximating the chromatic change in light as the sun moves from noon to sunset. Pay close attention to the color, angle and length of the figure's shadow and how it changes.

glorious shadows painters long for.

You'll hear professional artists & photographers occasionally refer to these narrow, early and late windows of color-filled sunlight as *The Golden Hour.*

They can be *incredible* to paint!

I should warn you though … if you opt to paint late in the day like I did, you'll quickly discover the sun doesn't care about your workout session.

It was startling the first time it happened … still, I should've known it was coming.

I was completely engrossed in my painting, when suddenly it's like somebody reached up and turned off the light … the really BIG light!

The sun had dropped behind the surrounding mountains, instantly plunging my scene into shadow.

Lesson learned …
pay attention to
start times.
Early morning
paint-outs will
have the shadows
growing ever
shorter (and
less dramatic/
appealing) while
you paint. The fact
is, the scene before

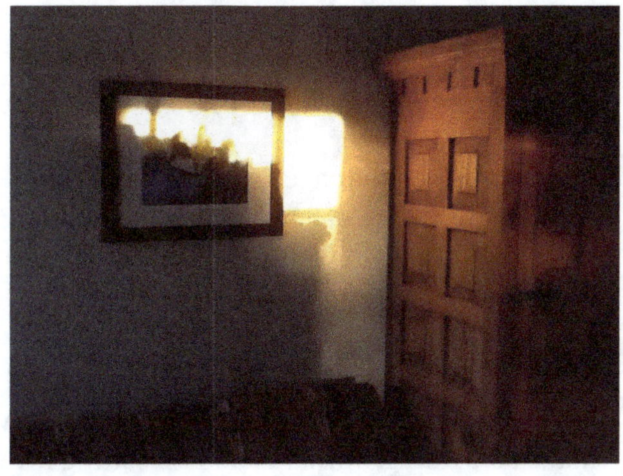

you is slowly degrading artistically every minute. But then nobody turns out the light on a morning session!

While writing this section I happened to look up in time to see the low afternoon sun powering through a studio window. The effect and color was almost exactly what I'm trying to describe.

You can readily see the yellow-orange sunlight against my studio's neutral grey wall.

RESILIENCE

I'm ashamed to admit that before all this, I used to be a real pantywaist while painting … hypersensitive to every minor mishap or glitch. This process fixed that.

I've painted on busy downtown street corners with homeless people inches away looking over my shoulder. And again,
I've had gear trashed by bad weather, etc. It all toughened me up in no time, making me more resilient than I could've ever imagined, regardless of the surrounding chaos or inevitable problems.

There were even times when I'd forgotten something critical, some MUST HAVE item left at home. I'd figure out a workaround, or just do without—and do my best.

One time I even managed to forget my tripod. I did say ONE TIME! I honestly couldn't believe it when it happened … I'd forgotten my TRIPOD!!! After a few minutes looking in all the "normal" places in my SUV, I began to maniacally dig through the mountains of junk in the back … NO TRIPOD!

I thought Mummert—you are SCREWED!! Now get over it and make something work. I ended up setting my pochade box on a small fold-up camp chair I'd found in the back of my SUV, and painted on my knees. Now that will help you to paint faster!

These days I tell people I can paint under just about any circumstances—except two. The first is high winds. High winds blow *everything* around ... turpentine, medium, brushes, umbrella, you name it.

The second is when someone walks up and begins trying to hold a conversation with me while I'm trying to paint (mentioned earlier).

Don't get me wrong; I get it, they're curious, fascinated by what I'm doing. They mean no harm. I just can't do it, for reasons already listed. I should add, I've actually seen other artists pull it off, this chat while you paint thing—but not me. I'm always a bit in awe of artists that can do it.

For me, there's no easy answer. If my wife happens to be along, she's usually great at politely running interference with curious onlookers.

OVER-CLEANING YOUR BRUSHES WHILE YOU PAINT

While you paint, try not to constantly clean your brushes with solvent. I know I'll get some flak on this, but before you write it off, ask yourself this simple question: where are John Singer Sargent and Anders Zorn's jars full of turpentine outdoors? Where were all their piles of used up rags? None of the old photos I've seen of both men show either.

The most one will typically see is a small medium cup hooked onto their palette somewhere, and maybe a rag or two nearby. To be honest, this was a huge revelation when someone told me about it. It's so out of synch with what we see everywhere in oil painting these days.

I'd already started to change my approach on this when I had the occasion to watch a live painting demo up near Los Angeles. A nationally recognized artist did a portrait from a live model in just over 2 hours—and only went through maybe five regular-sized paper towel *sheets* – yep, that's it! Only five individual paper towels were used to do an entire portrait!

He'd also limited the cleaning of his brush in a small jar of thinner nearby, to *maybe* three times. Even so, his color and values were clean and spot on.

Now compare that with most of us, our rolls of paper towels tucked under one arm and a hefty-sized can of thinner close by. Just sayin' … this "clean less" practice is something you might experiment with during your 30-minute, outdoor exercises.

Before leaving this topic, I should probably add that Anders Zorn was said to have told his students to use only three brushes: one for the darks, one for the middle values and one for the lights. Bottom line is, when we keep our values separated on our brushes that will automatically produce less brush cleaning while you work—fostering faster, more efficient painting.

Notes

Notes

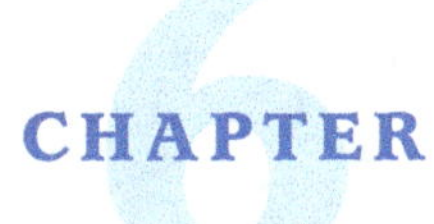

CHAPTER

Systemization & Increasing Speed Outdoors

*Each step of the process that we systemize
automatically increases our speed*

– S. C. Mummert –

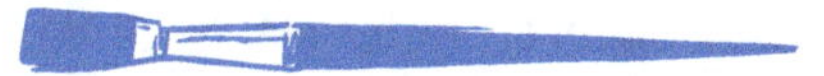

Representational artists are always judged first and foremost on
drawing. This is especially true with portraiture. An eye placed
too low on one side will invariably ruin a portrait for most people.
No matter how superbly the rest of the portrait's been painted, the
audience just won't be able to get past that low eye.

Of course landscapes aren't held to the same standard as portraiture.
Just the same, drawing is king. While I discuss increasing speed here,
understand I intentionally slow down during the drawing phase at the
beginning—because it matters.

This is probably a good time to share my personal hierarchy of artistic elements.

1. Drawing
2. Composition
3. Values
4. Edges
5. Color

Here's why they're in that order …

Drawing – (covered above)

Composition – This is the scaffolding, if you will, that everything's built upon. Yes, drawing is more important in the end. But just like the one low eye, a bad composition can *and will* ruin just about any work … landscape, still life or figurative.
Here are two of my videos on composition:
https://youtu.be/EnXMm9XbLF0?si=rZQckpcbgBlGE3uc
https://youtu.be/sq8Eyo-VMDg?si=PuKCJT60xrvRIHrv

Values – Correct values will make your paintings "sing".
Most people won't be able to put their finger on why they like your paintings. When your values are accurate … they'll just know it looks "right". When I first met Alex, I said that I wanted him to teach me color. He replied, "That tells me you don't understand values" and you know what, he was right.

Edges – Great edges usually separate an amateur from a pro. Many reading this will have no idea what I'm talking about when I bring up Edges. Suffice it to say, if the objects in your paintings all look like they're cut out with a pair of scissors, you need to begin learning about Edges. For those that'd like to learn more, I've written several articles on Edges that are available for free on my website -

Color – I could keep adding items to this list, but will stop with color. Here's why it's last: You can paint a portrait in virtually any color … even purple … and if it's drawn well, has a solid composition, good value structure and great edges—it'll work. Try it sometime and you'll see what I mean. Knowing this about Color actually gives us tremendous freedom for personal preference in our work.

The list is a mental hierarchy, not a painting process order. For example: settling on your scene and its composition will take place before everything else. While listed in fourth place, Edges are usually best addressed near the end of your painting.

Each of the elements should remain at play during the entire painting process. Nothing's ever off the table, not if it'll improve your painting. Corrective drawing never stops until your final stroke. Even basic compositional features can be strengthened or weakened near the end of your session.

With that in place, here are the steps I follow outdoors (after endless trial and [mostly] error).

1. *Locate a paintable scene. (Duh!)*

2. *Set up your gear.*

3. *Set the colors out on your palette.*

4. *Homogenize the consistency of your paints. Make them all the same viscosity.*

5. *Using a warm color, quickly apply a thin, stain-like wash over the entire canvas.*

6. *Decide on a Center of Interest or main focal point for the painting.*

7. *Quickly block in the large value patterns using the same color as the wash.*

8. *Begin to accurately draw in your scene in with your brush.*

9. *Place your Darkest Dark & Lightest Light (your value anchors). THINLY lay in your Darkest Dark. Use turpentine on a brush to erase down to your Lightest Light.*

10. *Begin laying in opaque color—working down from the top of your canvas.*

11. *Work thin in the early stages, getting thicker with your strokes as time passes.*

12. *When in doubt about a color—use grey at the correct value.*

13. *Work from dark to light.*

14. *Purpose to keep your dark areas thin, and light areas thicker and more opaque.*

15. *Save the most brilliant, chromatic and saturated color for the end.*

16. *Whenever possible, locate your Darkest Dark, Lightest Light, Hardest Edge and most Brilliant Color at your Center of Interest— to hold the eye of your viewer.*

OKAY, LET'S EXPAND ON THAT …

1. Locate A Paintable Scene

Find out where the "diamonds" are—then go ~~mine~~ paint them every day. - S. C. Mummert

Here's the deal: it's simply faster and more efficient if you return to the same location day after day, at least for a while. Time isn't wasted running all around, hunting for another "ideal" spot to paint each and every day.

In my case, the "Diamond Mine" happened to be just down the road from our home. It was a broad, dry riverbed surrounded by California Oaks. It wasn't glacial lakes in the High Sierras. But it was special in its own quiet way, and I actually came to love it.

Were I living closer to the ocean, I'd probably have picked a spot on the coastline. Again, it doesn't have to be someplace spectacular. It only needs to have enough variety to be interesting—to you. It's important to say here that you can paint the same scene within your Diamond Mine more than once—Monet did, you can too.

There's always more diversity in a location than we think, if we'll only look.

For example, I could simply paint the trunk of an oak tree as a study one day, or do a quick sketch of the clouds overhead the next. You get the idea. Again, the diamonds are right in front us, if we'll only look.

Immediately begin looking for what you might paint <u>*while you walk into your setting*</u>. On sunlit days, pay close attention to the direction that the sunlight's coming from. It'll help you find the most "paintable" scenes. Here're two illustrations to help you understand what I'm referring to.

Both diagrams are based on Frank Reilly's classic: *Four Basic Lighting Systems.* The first one's intended to show you how this might work while on location. Facing yourself directly toward the sun, look off to the right or left (roughly 15°) and you'll find yourself looking at what Reilly referred to as a *Rim Lit* scene(s). *Rim Lit* scenes naturally convey a sense of drama.

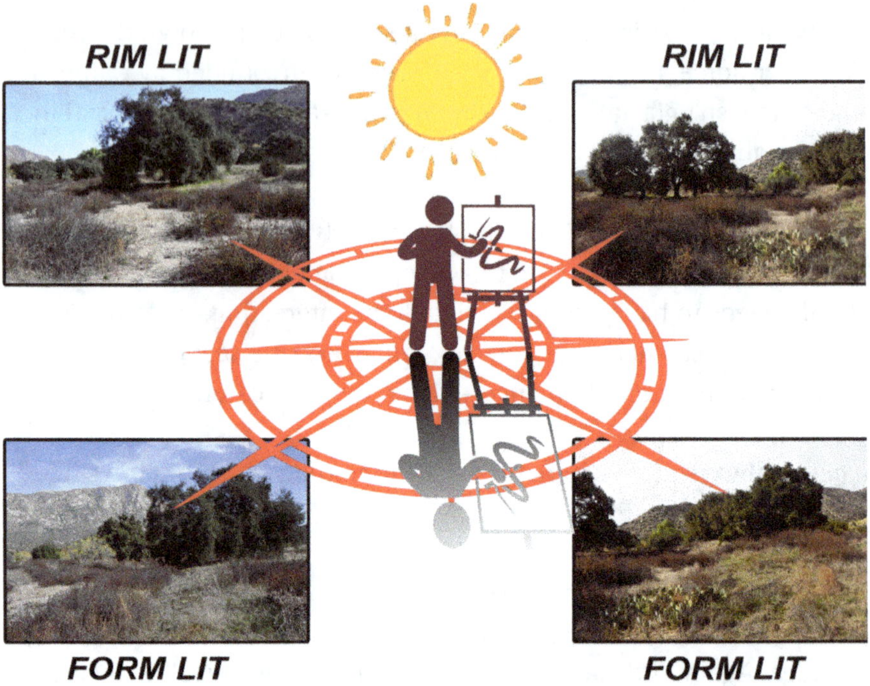

RIM LIT

RIM LIT

FORM LIT

FORM LIT

Next, spin yourself around 180°, turning your back squarely to the sun and once again look off about 15° to either side, your scene(s) will be *Form Lit. Form Lit* scenes frequently offer us great tonal structure to paint.

The second illustration here has been added for further clarity. It shows an artist's mannequin head (courtesy John Asaro) lit up using each of Frank Reilly's basic lighting classifications. The heads on the left (both outlined in red) are the two lighting formats I'm suggesting we focus on outdoors.

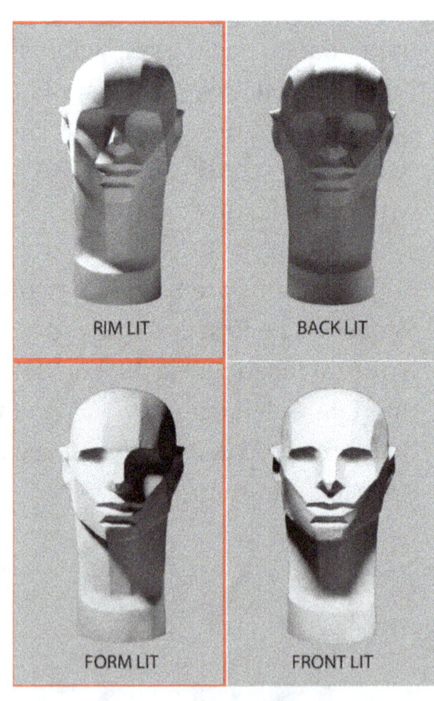

2. Set Up Your Gear

I've covered my feelings on this earlier under Muscle Memory. Bottom line: Find the most efficient way to set up your gear, then ruthlessly stick to it … until you find a method that works even better.

3. Consider Homogenizing Your Paints

Regardless of the oil paint manufacturer you use, you'll usually find varying degrees of thickness in your paints while squeezing them out. Some pigments seem to naturally default to being either thinner or thicker. You'll even find different paint thickness show up in tubes of the same color and from the same manufacturer—but created during different production runs. It's usually no big deal, that is, unless you're trying to paint fast. Then it can matter—a lot!

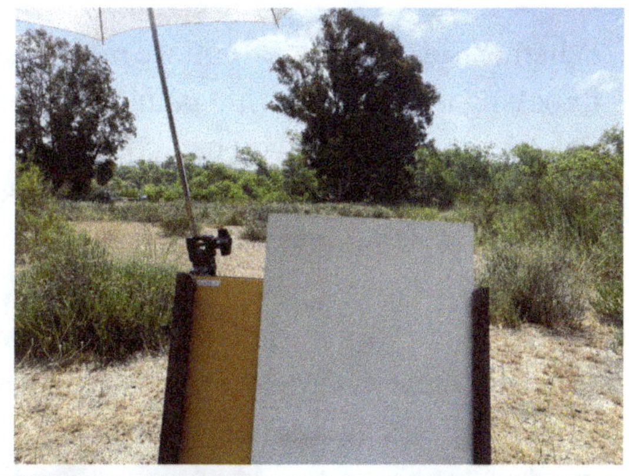

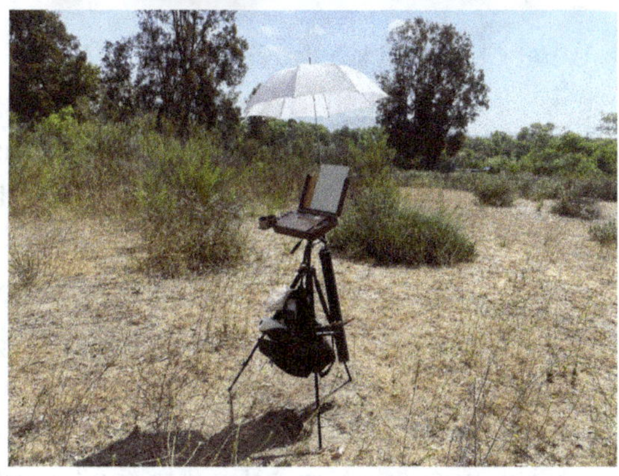

My gear all set up and ready

Here's my point, for the sake of speed, try to keep all the piles of paint on your palette the same viscosity.

The easiest solution is to add a little linseed oil into the stiffer piles of paint with your palette knife until all the piles match. The goal is for each pile of paint on your palette to feel identical whenever you put your brush into it.

Whether we realize it or not, we're repeatedly taking time to fix the annoying issue of differing paint thickness. Better to address it before you hit the timer—so you can effortlessly go from color to color while racing against the clock. After I began taking this simple extra step, I saw myself painting noticeably faster.

Famous New York illustrator Dean Cornwell used to say,
"When your White (paint) is the consistency of mayonnaise—
your painting's half done!"

What Cornwell was saying is that White (likely Flake White in his case) is notoriously thick … AND because it goes into virtually every other color—fixing it's consistency means not fighting stiff paint (again and again) while painting. Same idea.

In closing here, I should also mention there were times I'd set out the colors on my palette and "pre-homogenize" them back in the studio. It allowed me to slide the pochade box into my backpack, ready-to-go for the afternoon session. Once onsite, I'd quickly pull out the pochade box, affix it to the tripod's head, open the lid and immediately start painting.

Here're a couple shots using the palette knife to work linseed oil into a single pile of paint in the studio. Put the oil on your knife, to better control the quantity added.

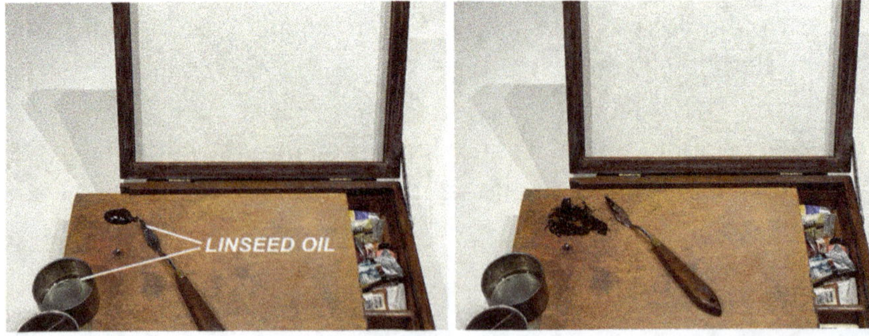

4. Stain Your Entire Canvas

Legendary commercial artist Haddon Sundblom used to
refer to the initial, raw white of his canvas as *"the enemy"*. Whenever
starting a new painting, the very first thing he'd do was stain
every inch of his canvas' surface using a thin transparent wash of
turpentine and oil paint.

Here are two 9x12 canvas
panels side by side. The
one on the right is new
and untouched.

The one on the left
has a light stain and
subsequent underpainting
on it—using Raw Umber.

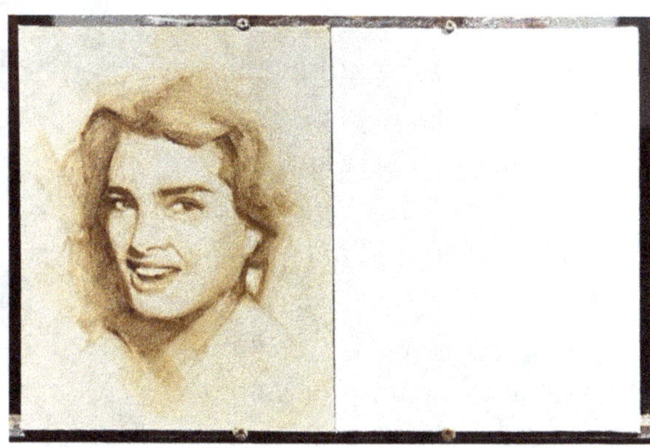

The term for this early, staining process is *Imprimatura*.
An *Imprimatura* quickly rids us of the white canvas; lends overall
harmony to the painting, and provides a much better starting point
for making all subsequent value decisions.

I typically dip a scrunched-up paper towel into my turpentine first,
then into the color I want to use, then make a few circular passes
on my palette to mix the two together—then quickly wipe down the
whole canvas. Like Sundblom, I use the same process in or out of the
studio, whenever I begin a piece.

Here's a shot of a plein air piece … after it's been stained with a quick
wash of Alizarin Crimson & Raw Umber

5. Quickly Block In Your Compositional Value Patterns

Probably the best way to describe the aggregate painting process
is to compare it with sculpting. A sculptor starts out with a lump of

clay, and begins work on the big stuff first—the BIG shape(s) and overarching design. As time passes, attention steadily moves towards ever-smaller elements. Minute details left for the end. Start Big—End Small.

Same thing with painting; the larger shapes and patterns are put down first. Block in the basic composition using shapes of light and dark (for more info go to Patterns of Light & Dark on my website - https://www.scmummert.com/ArticleDetail/10341)

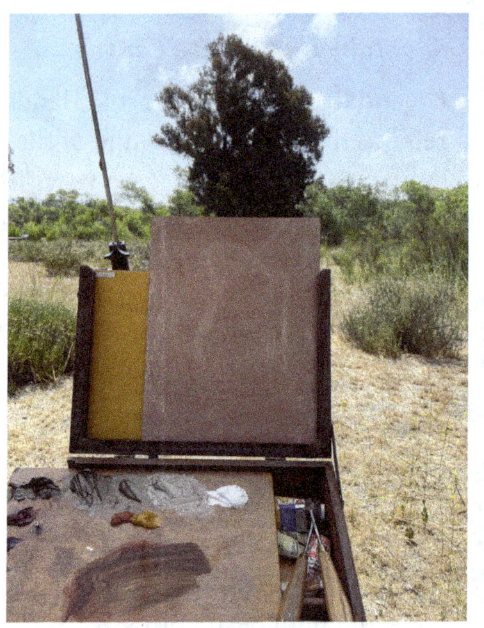

6. Begin To Accurately Draw In Your Scene

In the midst of the 30-minute time limit—this is where I slow down. Accurate drawing is at the Top of the List!

Okay, so you've wiped down your entire panel with thinned paint to get rid of the white. Then you quickly blocked in your patterns of light and dark. Now it's time to nail the drawing within your painting.

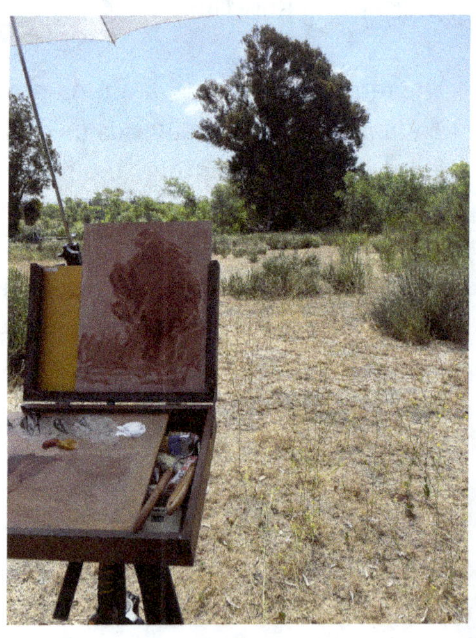

To do this: I frequently use two separate brushes … one to add paint, the other (using turp or thinner) to subtract and erase back where needed.

That's precisely how the underpainting shown earlier was done. It's similar to working in charcoal. Simply add and subtract pigment where you need to—until it looks right.

7. *Place Your "Value Anchors" EARLY*

One of the most important things you'll ever learn is understanding how unbelievably limited the value range of your oil paint is when compared to the world around you.

The only way we can hope to create something close to what we see in real life is by maintaining value *relationships.* We need to continually ask ourselves: *"How does this value compare with that one?"* It's ALL relative … nail your values, and you'll usually have a winner!

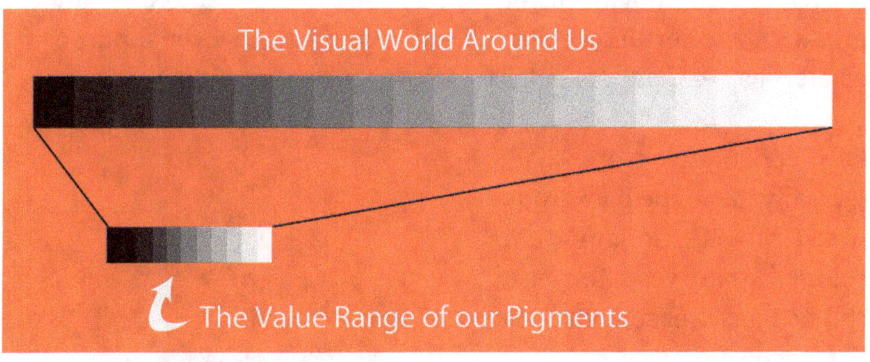

One of the best ways to influence your value decisions is by laying down your darkest dark and lightest light early. They'll be your absolutes … the top and bottom limits of the values you have to work with. *Every other paint stroke on your canvas will have a value somewhere between those absolutes of light and dark.*

8. Start Laying In Opaque Color

Whether in the studio or the great outdoors, I always try to work from my background *forward*.

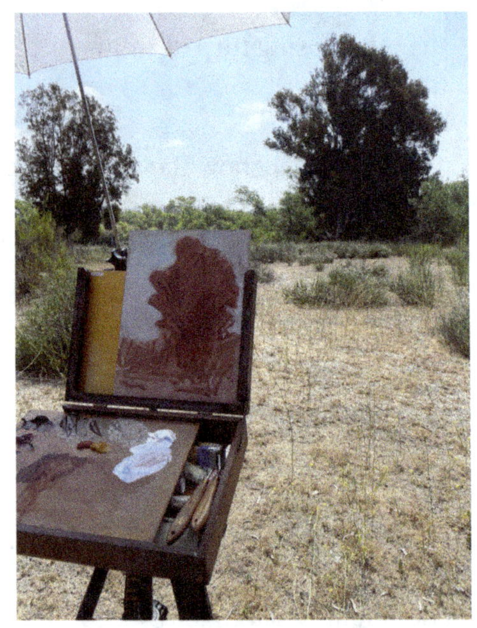

In a landscape, because the foreground is near the bottom of your canvas, that means laying in your first opaque color up near the top of your painting, and working downward.

Of course you can (and should) go back and forth while you paint.

It's just that working from your background forward automatically produces wonderful overlaps in form. Closer objects overlapping whatever's behind them helps us create an illusion of depth.

Even in figurative work, I'll typically lay in the background first. It provides an important color key that everything else can be harmonized with … like in this cowgirl piece.

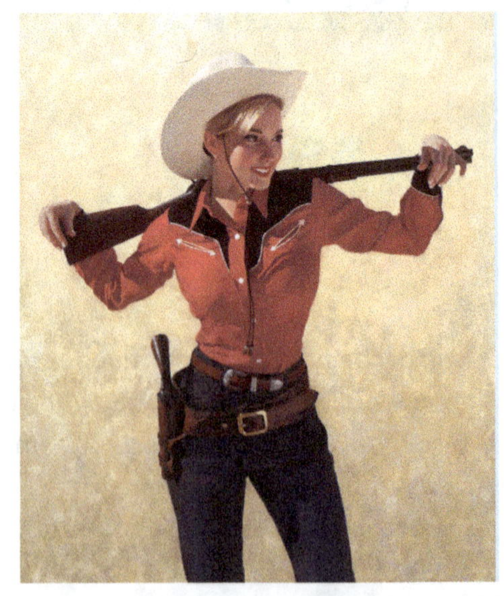

9. Purpose to Work From Dark to Light

As you work various areas in your painting, continually try to work from the darks to the lights.

That said, there'll simply be times where painting from dark to light won't apply.

For example, when we're laying in a final dark accent within a shadow.

10. Paint From Thin to Thick

Begin by painting thin, adding more opacity as you go … wrapping things up at the very end with your thickest strokes.

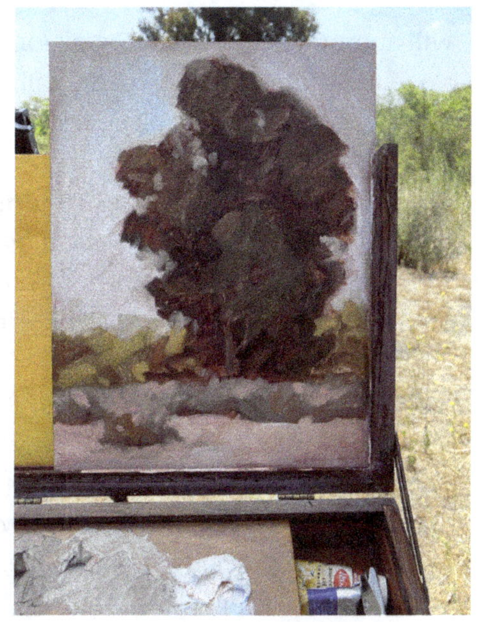

Beyond helping your form to "emerge", there's another great reason to start thin and end thick. If you start laying your paint on heavy at the beginning, it's often difficult to add more (and more) paint on top of the thick layers already in place.

Give it a try sometime—you'll see what I'm talking about.

So again, start thin, working ever thicker as you go. Near the end, laying it on thick where it counts.

There's also a technical reason to paint from thin to thick … *Ancient Oil Painting Maxim: Paint Fat Over Lean!*

That axiom actually covers several archival issues, to include: the use of oil mediums and the effective oil content within each pigment, as it comes from the manufacturer.

For our purposes, we'll only be applying it to the amount of paint you actually lay down. How thick is the paint? Thicker paint, by volume, will automatically have more oil (or fat) in it and will normally dry slower. A thin wash of oil paint will dry a lot faster than something that's been troweled in place with a palette knife.

This longevity guideline doesn't normally apply to single-session paintings. That's because everything's getting laid down at just about the same time. However, working on a single painting over several days (or weeks) is a *completely* different story.

Here's why: if you happen to apply some thick (slower drying) paint in an area one day, then show up the following day and add some thin paint over yesterday's (thicker) work, you're virtually guaranteed to see cracking in the paint later on. *Cracks in oil paint are almost always the result of placing faster drying paint over slower drying paint.*

11. *When In Doubt Regarding A Color In Your Scene— Use A (Pre-Mixed) Grey*

There'll be times when you're painting away and suddenly realize *you have absolutely no idea what the exact color of the thing is you're trying to paint!*

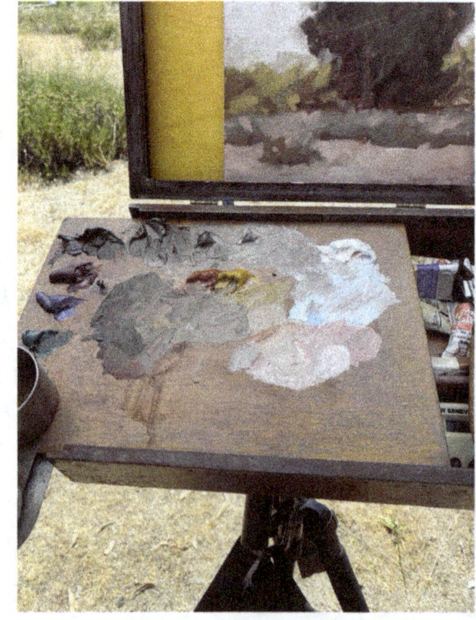

When that happens (and it will), consider the temperature of the light hitting your scene. The color of light affects everything in it. For instance, warm light regularly produces cooler shadows—like the shaded area under a tree.

On an overcast day, where the light's rather cold—the same shadowed region under a tree will appear comparatively warm against the areas out receiving the cooler daylight.

Knowing stuff like that helps A LOT! Still … there'll be times you can't figure out what color to use. In those instances, I suggest you grab a grey of the correct value, paint it in—and move on. Again, like Walt Disney used to say, *"Keep moving forward!"*

I should add, don't be surprised as the painting progresses, that you suddenly know the right color to use where a grey was plugged into earlier.

That's because *painting is (again) entirely about relationships*. Adjacent colors invariably help us identify the actual color of something—like holding up a black sock to a navy blue one.

As time passed, I began setting out an abbreviated row of warm greys in successive values up near the top of my palette.

The idea of using a set of greys arranged by value actually came from my studio training. They make short work of finding a grey to use in situations like this. I discuss pre-set greys in more detail in Chapter 8 - *SETTING OUT A 5-VALUE GREY SCALE.*

12. Keep your darks thin, and your lights thick and opaque

Thinly painted, transparent shadows recede. Opaque, thickly painted passages in the light tend to advance. Rembrandt is the quintessential example of this approach. He really piled on the paint when something was in the light.

13. Try to save the most saturated color for the "end"

Contrasting elements can really help bring power to your paintings. Old against new, light against dark, sharp against dull, tall against short—and fully saturated color surrounded by grey.

I mention that here, because I habitually hold down Chroma in my paintings at the beginning of the process, adding more and more saturation as time passes. This technique sets things up for painting in the brightest color(s) near the end … ideally at (or near) the painting's center of interest.

Which brings me to …

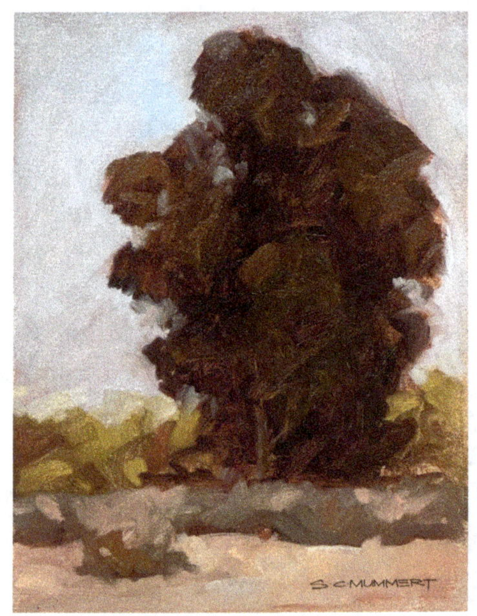
30 Minute Sketch

14. *Whenever possible, place your Darkest Dark, Lightest Light, Hardest Edge and most Saturated Color at or near your Center Of Interest.*

Ideally, even a 30-minute sketch has everything in it, at least that should be the goal.

Let's see …
- A well-balanced composition, with strong patterns of Light and Dark
- Directional features—designed to draw the viewer into your painting
- Closed corners (whenever possible) to hold your audience in your scene
- A wide variety of edges ranging from completely lost to razor sharp
- Color harmony
- Variety in paint texture
- Bold, confident brushwork

And then, last but not least: a strong *Center of Interest*.

Ask yourself, where's the one place—*the most important place*—in the painting where I want my audience to look? What's the *Center of Interest*? Of course only you can decide what and where that is ... but you do need to decide.

When we identify our Center of Interest, there are visual elements we can put to use, to help hold our viewer's attention on that single (most important) spot. Like the heading says, they're your *Darkest Dark*, your *Lightest Light*, your *Hardest Edge* and your *Most Saturated Color*.

I'll use one of my studio pieces to illustrate what I'm talking about. I've added two images of the same piece for greater clarity—one with a bunch of explanatory arrows and labels, the other without.

Again, here's a YouTube video of mine on where I use the same painting and diagram to explain these concepts in greater detail - https://www.youtube.com/watch?v=sq8Eyo-VMDg

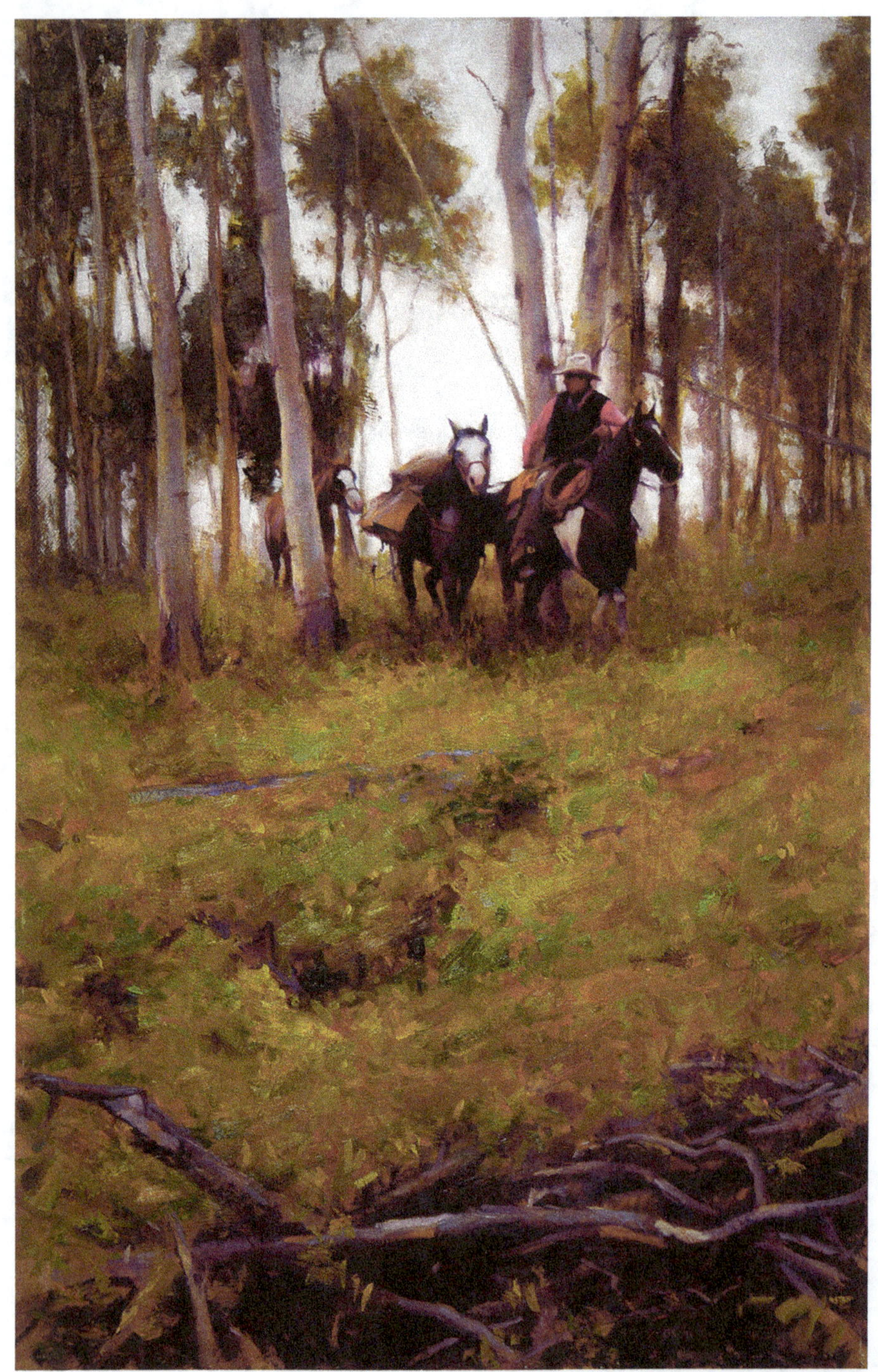

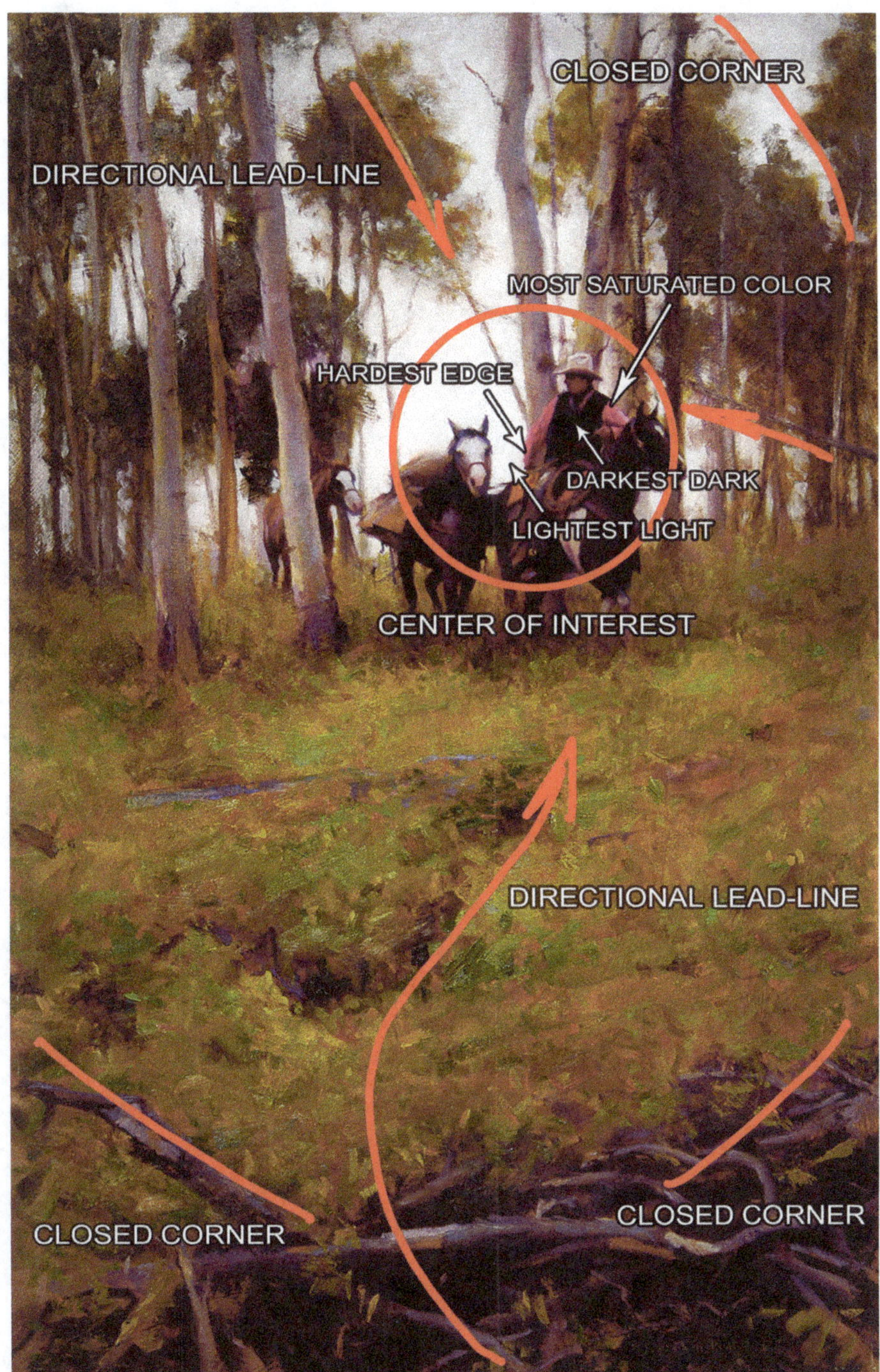

CLOSED CORNER
DIRECTIONAL LEAD-LINE
MOST SATURATED COLOR
HARDEST EDGE
DARKEST DARK
LIGHTEST LIGHT
CENTER OF INTEREST
DIRECTIONAL LEAD-LINE
CLOSED CORNER
CLOSED CORNER

Notes

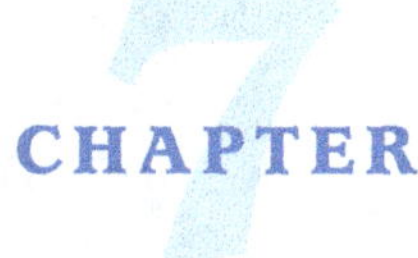

CHAPTER

The Afterburners

*Virtually all progress has its roots
in a functioning feedback loop.*

– S. C. MUMMERT –

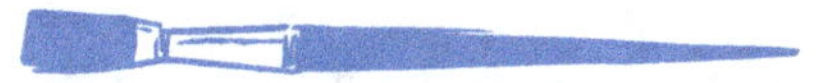

FEARLESS EXPERIMENTATION -
THE SECRET TO ACCELERATED LEARNING

Weeks turned into months ... with an absolute river of Frisbee's painted and tossed out along the way. But then each trashcan reject drove a stake deeper into the heart of my real enemy— the Fear of Failure. Honestly, it's every artists' (and more than a few non-artists) fundamental enemy.

When I finally recognized how much fear had been holding me back over the years, it was like a veil was pulled back. The fact is: *failures are lessons.* I'm going to repeat that: *failures are lessons.* Man, it took me a loooong time to wrap my head around that powerful truth.

But once I did, I thought … why not start experimenting with a BUNCH of stuff outdoors?! I have nothing to lose—NOTHING! It's all good! It'll be one big, open-air/art laboratory! Sure, I might crash a lot, but even the Frisbees are making me better! I can try out a zillion new colors, every kind of brush I want … different painting mediums and pre-textured canvas panels—you name it! The lid was off! It was all one BIG, GRAND ADVENTURE … so why not go exploring!

And, so it began. If I wanted to try out a new color, I'd just bring it along and squeeze it out along with the other pigments to see how it worked. If I liked what I saw that day, I'd leave it on my palette for a week or so, and watch how things went. It's amazing how quickly I got to know a new color after painting with it nearly every day for a week.

I'd always been impressed with the effects I'd seen other artists produce with a palette knife. Of course I'd never used one … they were too erratic and unpredictable. You know—SCARY! I finally thought how dumb, give one a shot Mummert, just like everything else. So I casually tossed one into my outdoor gear one day and gave it a whirl all week long. I came to love it and use one all the time now. Again … Accelerated Learning!

You name it … nothing should be off the table. In fact, I'd say the scarier something is the better! It's probably something you've been avoiding and NEED to learn! Pick something, ANYthing, and try it out. BE BOLD! If you don't like it—it's no big deal. The important thing is you've learned and grown in knowledge from the experience. *Put the pedal to the metal and start to fearlessly test stuff out.*

I'm going to keep repeating this, because we BOTH need to hear it again and again. The real heart of the system is for us, *all of us*, to do the unthinkable—to actually recognize failure is an inescapable by-product of rapid growth. It shouldn't be a surprise we're wickedly averse to failing. Grownups are particularly conditioned to avoid it at all costs. I know I was.

It all started when we were quite young. Most kids are enthusiastically rewarded for any and all success. A baby speaking their first word, or what their parents *THINK* is a word, usually triggers oceans of praise. First steps, more positive reinforcement ... *GREAT JOB Johnny! Keep it up!!!* First time riding a bicycle without training wheels, *YAY! I knew you could do it!!!* ... on and on. By the way, that's precisely how it should be.

Success *should* be rewarded. Here's the problem ... over time we forget that as youngsters we spoke *mountains* of gibberish before our first "word" slipped out. We fell a zillion times before we could finally walk. Here's the deal, if we ultimately succeed at something, we eventually forget the failures—and we should. It's normal and healthy.

Babe Ruth's stunning record of home runs eclipses the fact that he was the reigning strikeout king! There were times he'd swing so hard while missing the ball that he'd actually fall down. Can you imagine the public humiliation he endured? The raunchy catcalls and jeers? In the end, none of those painful failures really mattered. Only his tremendous success is remembered today.

He was once asked about all the times he'd swung and missed. He said, *"Every strikeout brings me closer to the next home run"*. He knew if he did his best and gave it everything he had, each and every time, his gritty persistence would eventually pay off ... and it did.

I guess I share all of that, because even if you've been painting for a while I'm going to ask that you begin relentless experimentation. Start exploring your materials and mediums with fresh eyes. Take a brand new look at your palette's current color scheme … or the brand, style and size of the brushes you use—or don't use. No sacred cows … nothing should be exempt from scrutiny.

That said, here are some suggestions …

- *Do an entire painting with a single one-inch brush.*
- *Try using only Filberts for a period of time, then only Long Flats—and then only Brights. What is it about each brush that you like, or dislike?*
- *If you only use synthetic brushes, think about trying out natural brushes with Hog, Sable or Badger.*
- *If you've only used natural fiber brushes, consider giving synthetic brushes a shot.*
- *Remove Black from your palette, and see how you do.*
- *Do several paintings with only Alizarin Crimson, Cerulean Blue, Cadmium Orange and Titanium White—and see what happens.*
- *Give Ivory Black, Yellow Ochre, Thalo Green, Alizarin Crimson and Titanium White a shot for a few days.*
- *Limit yourself to Cadmiums, Ultramarine Blue and Titanium White on another day.*
- *Show up one day with only Ivory Black, Raw Umber, Cad Red Light, Yellow Ochre & Titanium White … and see what happens.*
- *Add and subtract colors from your palette at will—week after week.*
- *Try using a different painting medium every week for a while.*
- *Then switch over to using no medium at all … just Turpentine or Turpenoid.*
- *Begin experimenting with a palette knife while you paint.*

- *Try painting an entire week using only a palette knife. Then switch the next week to a completely different palette knife and see how it goes.*
- *Turn your timer off (if you've been using one), and do a painting using only 100 brush strokes—period. Count each one, and you'll make each one count.*
- *Then do another using only 50 brush-strokes. Focus on saying the most you can, with the fewest strokes possible.*
- *Study edges in Anders Zorn or Haddon Sundblom's work; then begin to apply what you've learned in this week's paintings. Again, here's a link to several articles I've written on edges - https://www.scmummert.com/articles*
- *Set your timer down to 20 minutes one day—then up to 40 the next. Pay close attention to how you responded to the reduced, and expanded times.*
- *Texture your canvas panels beforehand with Gesso, then watch the effects you're able to create with knife and brush.*
- *Texture several panels with Gesso—using only horizontal brush-strokes.*
- *Then Gesso several more panels using only vertical textured brush-strokes.*
- *Then take a palette knife (before the Gesso's dried) and create random, irregular effects on your canvas.*
- *Paint only vertical (portrait orientation) pieces for a week.*
- *Pick one color (one hue) … and then mix some of it into every other pile of pigment on your palette before painting— add no more than 1/3.*
- *Try the above experiment using a different color each day.*

The opportunities for growth can seem almost limitless. That's really one of the greatest secrets I discovered along the way. What we're essentially setting up here is an accelerated, never-ending way to develop as an artist … a place where failures are nothing more than growing pains.

That revelation can free us up to expand our painterly knowledge and ability at a new, breathtaking pace.

I want you to repeatedly test your artistic skills on brand new things—over and over again, all without fear. If you mess up … and you will … so what? Big deal! Frisbee that baby and take another shot at it. Stay at it and don't give up. Again, persistence is an awesome force in the universe. The only time we're really beaten is when we give up. Just like a toddler that's eventually up and running around everywhere, you will get it. It's just how things are set up in this world of ours.

I call it *cycle time*. We've zeroed in on reducing the time between each cycle … between each learning experience. *Perfect practice makes perfect*. Keep practicing *perfectly*. Even if some paintings are losers and others winners—like the toddler repeatedly falling down, they're all adding up to become part of a fast, and ultimately positive learning process. There'll be days it won't feel like you're winning … but trust me; if you give it your all, the road to success just got shorter.

Step 7

Don't give up

Author Napoleon Hill was given the unique privilege of personally interviewing Thomas Edison and Henry Ford over the course of several years. While writing about these two titans of American industry, Hill concluded the single greatest reason for their success was a complete refusal to give up, in spite of continual setbacks. Perseverance pays off!

Notes

Notes

Beyond The 30-Minute Workouts

There's always "one more thing" to learn –

– STEVE JOBS –

As I'd mentioned earlier, my 30-minute sketches eventually led me into regular Plein Air painting—where on the average, 60-90 minutes were spent on a small piece. In this section, I'll cover a few of the technical advances and discoveries from that expanded season.

- The Reilly Palette & outdoor 5-value grey scale
- Get mad! You might be amazed at how well you paint!
- Color harmonies outdoors
- Interchange

THE REILLY PALETTE

Born in 1906, Frank Reilly taught art in New York City until his untimely death in January of 1967. A brilliant instructor, during the late 1950's, his students were creating the cover artwork for three out of every four paperback books.

I mention that because I was originally trained up in the *Reilly System* for my studio work. At the core of his method was a specialized, "controlled" palette—often referred to as *The Reilly Palette*. Basically, the artist's colors are all pre-arranged according to value within a rectangular, grid-like format.

Historical references suggest that the palette, with its unique design may have originated with Leonardo Da Vinci. Versions of it were used extensively throughout Europe, before coming to America around the early 1900's.

It's been given a bunch of different names over the centuries, none of which matter at this point. What matters is the overall brilliance of the concept. It offers almost complete command of the craft of oil painting.

That said, it's not for everyone. Former Reilly student John Asaro doesn't use a controlled palette, preferring to use a loose palette— and he paints beautifully. Ditto for Anders Zorn, John Singer Sargent, Norman Rockwell and countless others that all produced brilliant paintings.

Personally, I can paint with either a *loose* or *controlled* palette. I do find that a controlled palette (after setting it up) allows me to paint faster, and achieve smooth transitions with ease, particularly in figurative work.

For now, I'll simply be introducing it to those who've never seen it before. Here's a quick shot of a Reilly-style palette with its pre-mixed (by me) colors all laid out and ready to use ...

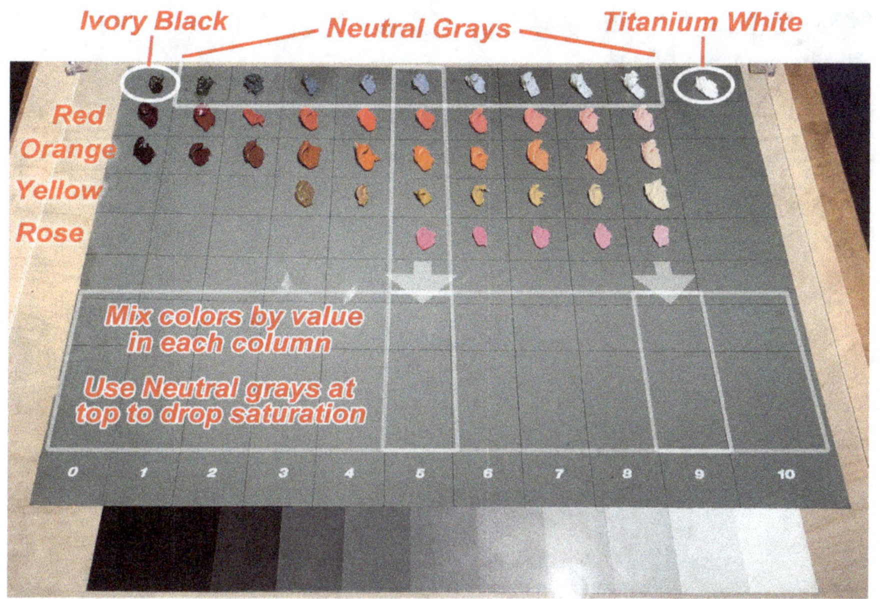

In case you're curious, that's clear, tempered glass placed over middle-value grey paper with a value scale down near the bottom—all resting on 3/8" plywood.

The palette and Reilly's accompanying system could easily fill another book.

The reason I share a picture of the palette here, is so that you'll better understand the "how and why" I arrived at my own outdoor palette configuration. (If you're interested in learning more about *The Reilly Palette*, here's a link to my YouTube video on it - https://www.youtube.com/watch?v=LNxz11P8yDg)

Ultimately, the Reilly palette came to influence how I set up my own outdoor palette. As you can see, it has an abbreviated value scale of (warm) greys laid out across the top.

Surprisingly, good old Darwin Duncan told me that Edgar Payne used to do the same thing. He'd personally watched Payne

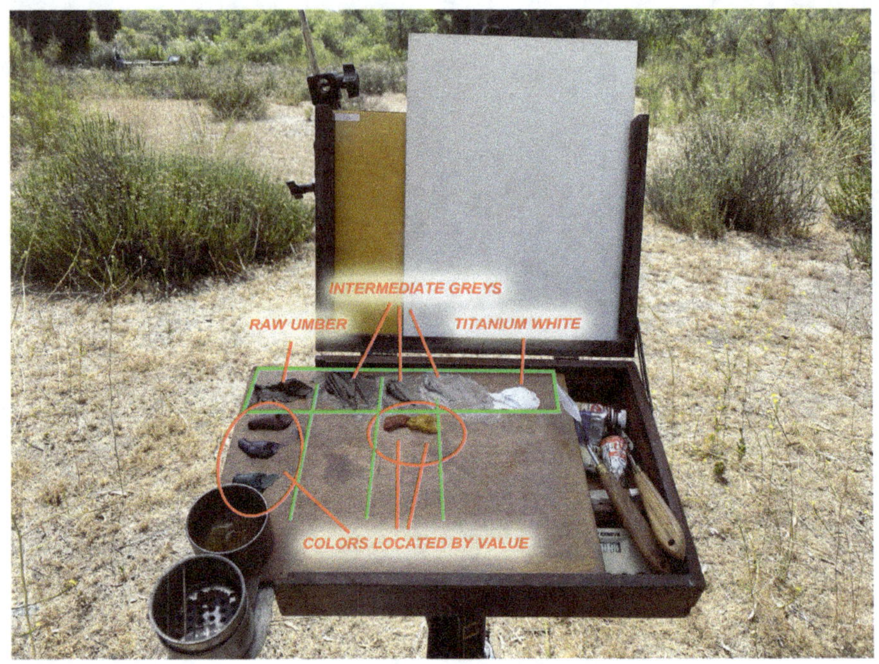

repeatedly set out a row of value-based greys right across the top of his palette. Payne would use a dark violet—rather than the Raw Umber I'm using here. You can see in the earlier illustration, that the original Reilly palette used ivory black and titanium white to produce the row of greys (or "neutrals" as Reilly would call them) up top.

Here's why a scale of sequential greys across the top is so fabulous: one of the hardest things to do, is to <u>quickly and predictably de-saturate a color from its raw "out-of-the-tube" state</u>. Mixing in a preset grey (of the right value - as needed) to regulate saturation solves that problem beautifully.

If the color you're trying to create looks too saturated (or chromatic), just reach up for a grey of similar value and mix it in as necessary. Done! It's important to add, that using a single greying agent (color) throughout the painting process will also automatically add harmony.

The rest of the colors (Alizarin Crimson, Ultramarine Blue, Viridian, Terra Rosa & Yellow Ochre) are all situated on the palette according to <u>value—not temperature</u> or relational harmony.

SETTING OUT A 5-VALUE GREY SCALE

Now that I've shown you a row of abbreviated greys in use, I should probably take a few minutes and show you how to create your own.

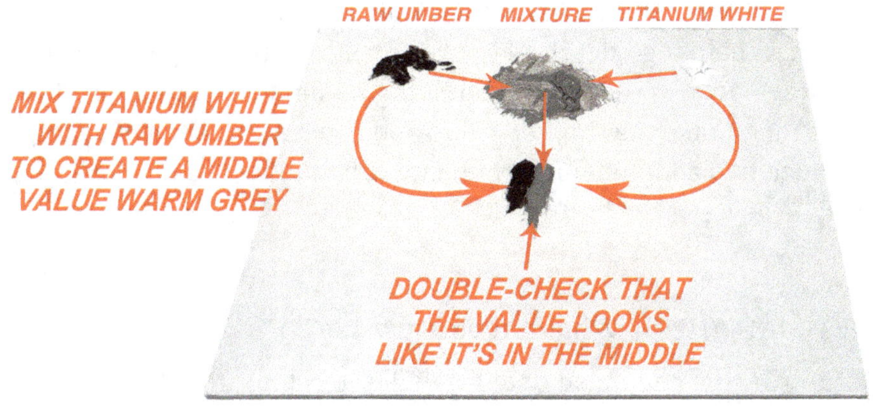

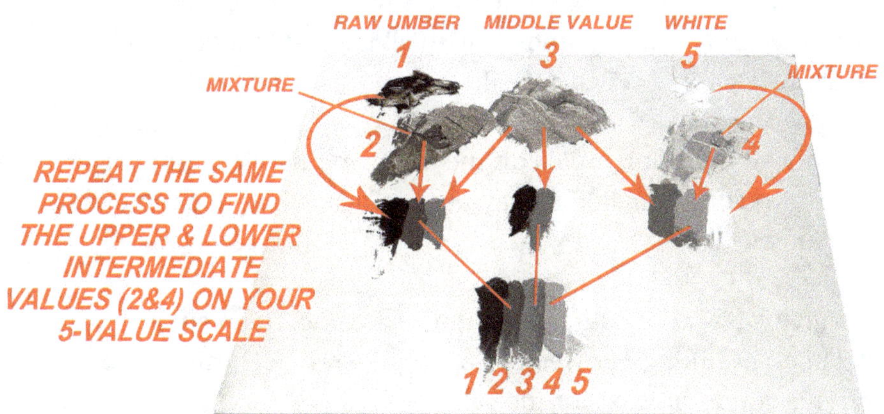

By the way, what I'm about to share was taught to me by one of my instructors over 40 years ago. It's a quick and simple method to make a "basic 5-value scale". You can set out this scale on your palette before heading out, or while standing outdoors in a field—I've done both.

Once you do it a couple times, you'll find it only takes a few minutes. That's largely because you're really only creating three intermediate values. Titanium White and Raw Umber (situated at opposite ends of the scale) are straight from the tube.

Here are the quick steps:

Using Raw Umber and Titanium White, I simply take the two and mix them together until I have something that appears to be halfway between the two. I'm creating my middle value. Once I've done that, I take that middle value and use it in the same way to produce two additional intermediate values, above and below. Easy-Peasy!

GET MAD! (HUH? What did you just say?!!)

A funny thing happened one day while standing atop the sandstone cliffs in La Jolla. I'd been doing these longer, "more finished" outdoor pieces and all of a sudden I realized that I was somehow getting stuck—AGAIN!! Like I'd landed on a "Mini-Plateau" of sorts! NOOOOO!!!!!

Because I had some miles on me at this point, I thought: It's fear … trying to sneak its way back in again (yes, it can be that pernicious!).

To give a bit more context, around that time, the plein air pieces I'd been cranking out week after week were beginning to look pretty good—at least for me.

BUT they still weren't where I wanted to be. Not really. You know, success can be a funny thing. If we're not careful, it'll lead us right into a kind of "safety zone", a place of comfort. "Hey, it's working! Leave it alone!" I thought NOOOOO! … all of a sudden I got a little

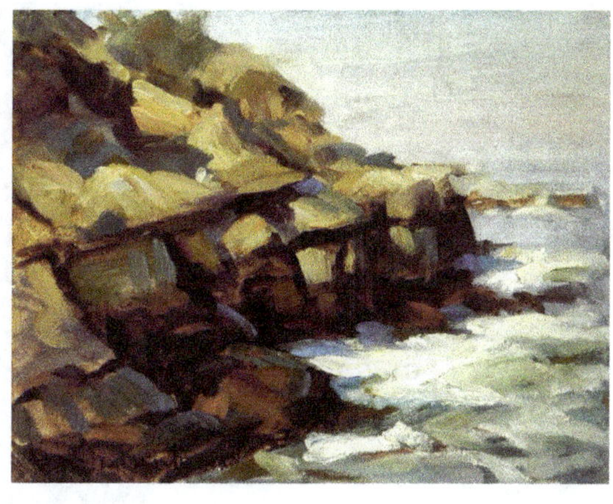

mad at myself, for being such a chicken. Especially after all of the time, money and effort I'd put in!

So right then and there, I marched down the rocky cliffs closer to the waves and slammed out this piece in record time! I'm not saying it's a masterpiece. I AM saying it was a breakthrough painting for me at the time.

I gotta say, it's pretty remarkable what we can accomplish when we're mad. We suddenly become fearless, bolder … maybe even a bit reckless! At least that's how I painted that day—and you know what, it worked!

Thought I'd pass that along, if you suddenly find yourself stuck like I did! When I closed the lid on my pochade box I knew I'd just experienced an abrupt and wonderful step forward.

INTERCHANGE

Interchange can take place in color and/or value. It's basically a form of gradient that repeatedly occurs in Nature. Stunning sunsets frequently present value and color *Interchange* effects simultaneously.

We have an example of
Interchange taking place in
the colors of theses Firestick
plants.

It's somehow visually
hardwired into us to love
the look of an *Interchange*.
Look for them and then
use them.

When applied properly—
they'll add beauty to
your paintings.

COLOR HARMONY

Have you ever seen
a painting where the
colors all seem harsh
and unbelievably raw?
We all have. That almost
never happens in nature.
Gorgeous color harmonies
abound outdoors—if only
we'll look.

They'll casually show up in
the granite face of a rock,
or in the peeling bark of a
eucalyptus tree ... or sneak
up on you while you're
walking along the seashore
near a tide-pool.

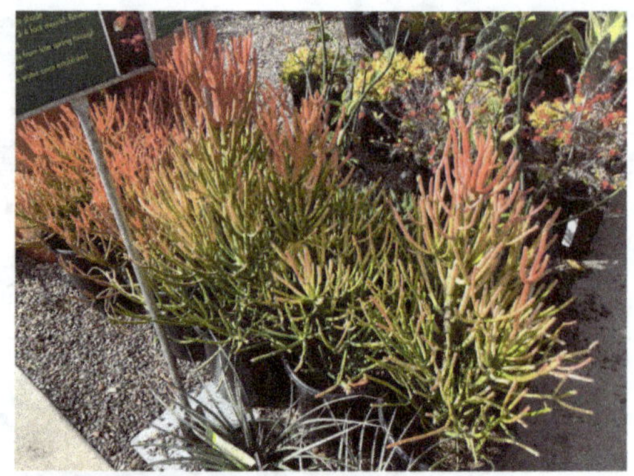

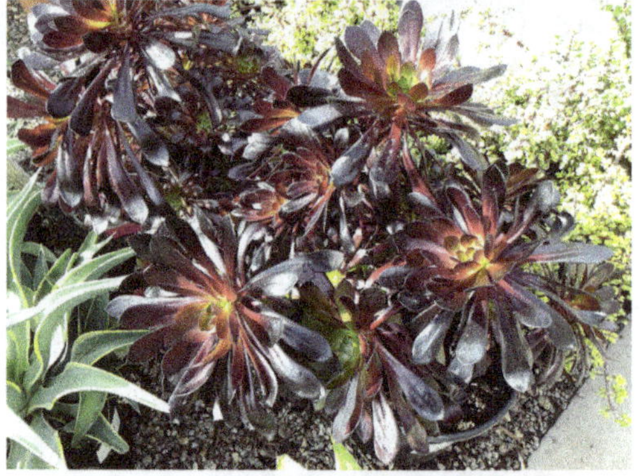

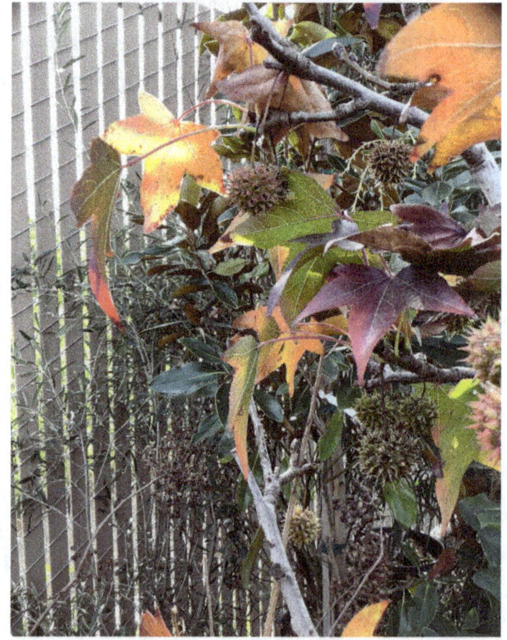

In fact, while writing this section, I went with my wife to a local nursery. She was busy buying some plants, so I began looking around.

It was December here in San Diego, but examples of nature's sublime color harmonies were everywhere. Here're a couple quickie shots I snapped to give you an idea of what I'm talking about.

I'd suggest whenever possible, you take time and photograph the various color harmonies you run into. Or better yet, capture it with oil paint when possible.

Over time you'll build up your own library of naturally occurring harmonies that can be used later.

I also suggest you start having a little fun and experiment creating your own harmonious color arrangements using the colors on your palette. You'll be amazed at what you can come up with.

If you do play around, as I'd mentioned earlier, try adding a small amount of one color into every other pile of paint on your palette.

Payne suggests keeping the additive color amount to under a third. More than that and we risk reducing the other pigments' identities too much.

I'll close with an article I wrote years ago regarding a color theory we don't hear much about these days. It really is quite remarkable.

THE ANALOGOUS / COMPLEMENTARY COLOR THEORY

What I'm about to share here won't be for everyone. There'll simply be those who haven't much time for this approach to color.

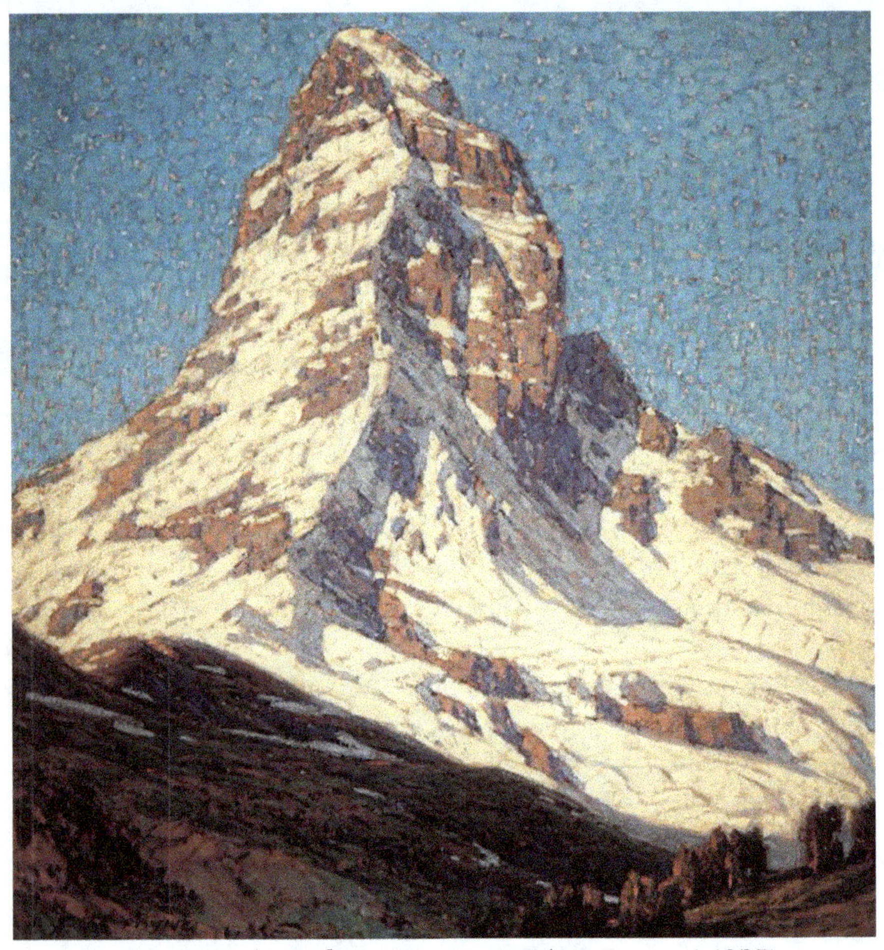

The Matterhorn from Zermatt - Edgar Payne (c1923)

If that's you, please know I understand and wish you the best. The enormous number of color theories within art, are very much open to one's own personality and preference.

Though rarely applied openly in my own work these days, this concept is there, like a computer program running quietly in the background … continually influencing how I paint and take in the world about me.

Okay, here we go …

A bunch of stuff came together about the time this was passed along to me. Roughly thirty years ago, I was busy spending a zillion hours painting outdoors, had recently been introduced to the Early California Impressionists *and* had one of America's top artists staying with us.

Several days before he was to fly home, my painter friend sat down and began to tell me about (what he called) - *The Analogous/ Complementary Color Solution*. I think he knew it would be a great fit for me at the time. And he was right. It immediately began to make more sense out of the colors I'd been seeing outdoors and helped answer a few questions I'd had regarding several Early California Impressionist paintings.

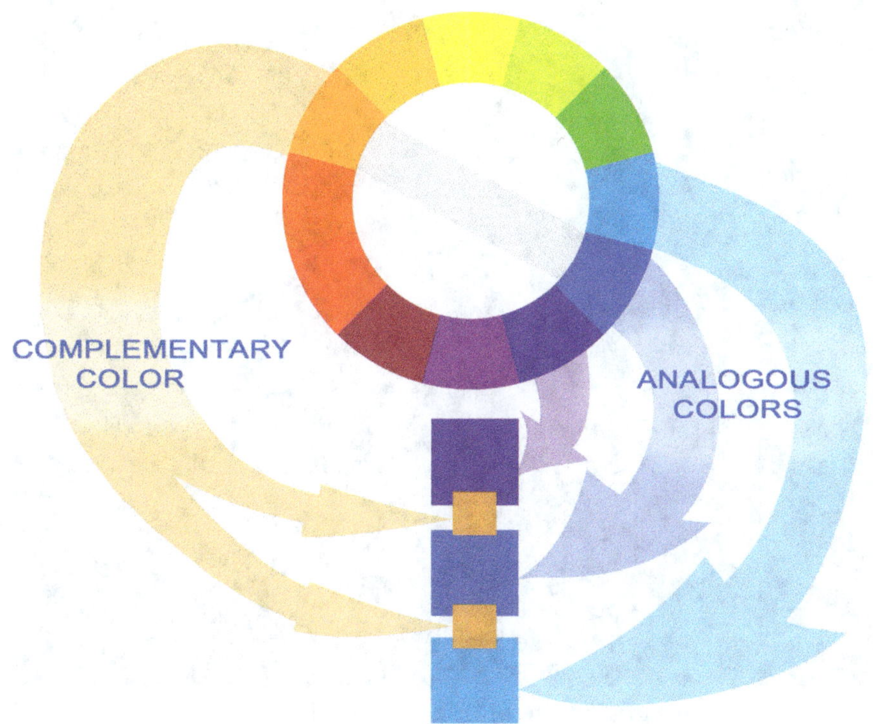

I should add, the paintings shown to help illustrate my points are somewhat exaggerated examples of the theory's use. That isn't to say they're not breathtaking pieces of art—because they are.
It's only that more understated (and equally beautiful) versions of its application would be correspondingly less obvious in relating the information.

I've attempted to reproduce the diagram drawn for me so long ago. In this instance, the illustration's colors loosely correspond to those found in the Matterhorn's sky.

Here we have three analogous (or related) "blues", woven together with a muted variation of their complement—orange. Those I've shared this concept with, over the years, are often surprised at the range of color trees seem to suddenly have ... particularly

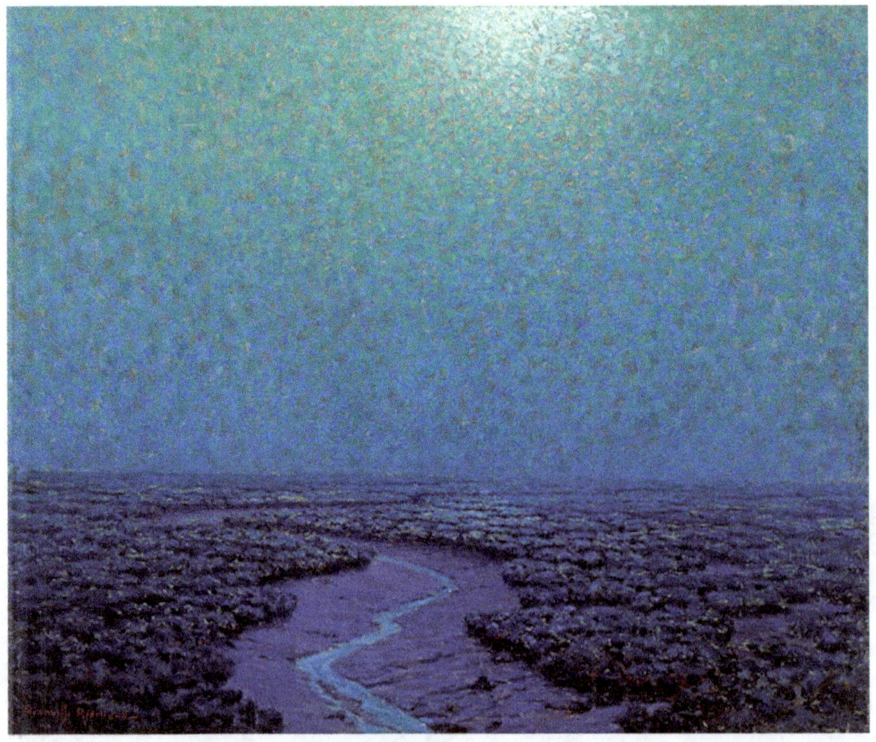

Moonlight on the Marsh - Granville Redmond.

the reds. (By the way, if you look, you'll see Payne's tree-filled foreground has red in it)

Here's my take on why this looks so fabulous … at least to me. Analogous colors are quite gorgeous in their own right. That's one reason why a rainbow seems so glorious. Each color is directly related to, and harmonious with, the one directly beside it.

Here's the rub, the receptors in our eyes can, and often do, become oversaturated with color—including our harmonious/analogous hues.

I suspect almost everyone reading this has at some point, been given a white card with a bright red dot on one side. You were probably asked to stare closely at the red dot for a short time, and then told to quickly turn the card over and see what's there. Usually, the image of a green dot (the red dot's complement) materialized on the card's reverse, blank white surface … an optical mirage.

Here's the point: whether we know it or not, our eyes automatically resist oversaturation … regularly setting in motion the same internal phenomena experienced during our red-dot/green-dot card test.

That inner-ocular response should happen precisely the same way when we're looking at a section of vivid green outdoors—but it doesn't, not always. The subtle reds, frequently knit among Nature's various greens help us out. They provide visual islands of rest, as it were … often reducing the need for our eyes to react. Pretty amazing.

One last point … *the saturation of the complementary color should usually be held down*—at or below the saturation of the (more abundant) analogous colors around it. In both the diagram and our painting examples, the warmer complement has been muted against the analogous/cooler hues.

You should know that there are countless variations of this effect to be found in the world of art. So please understand, this is a very basic introduction.

A parting suggestion: If you happen to give this a try, you'll probably find that wet-into-wet is the best way to begin experimenting with this. The existing, underlying wet paint will automatically help harmonize your efforts.

FINAL THOUGHTS

Though this book's a bit short, for many readers there'll be a lot here to digest. I suggest it be read several times, and taken along in your vehicle while out painting.

Though terribly imperfect, it's exactly what I desperately needed so long ago. Again, what's contained here forever changed me as an artist. My hope is that it does the same for a few determined souls. As for me, I'm still trying to get better as an artist—every day—using other techniques based on this same concept.

- Remember, your personal artistic growth is vastly more important than any single painting. Significant gains come when we begin to focus more on us the artist, than on the art.

- Purpose to overcome the fear of failure. "Do the thing you fear and the death of fear is certain." - *Ralph Waldo Emerson*

- Eat the elephant one bite at a time … consistent small steps—over time—can work miracles.

Notes

I can be reached through my website
https://www.scmummert.com

Thank you, and God Bless!
S. C. Mummert